Tax Guide 505

GOING
INTO
TAX COURT

by

Holmes F. Crouch
Tax Specialist

Published by

Allyear Tax Guides

20484 Glen Brae Drive
Saratoga, CA 95070

ISBN 0-944817-33-5

LCCN 96-84939

Printed in U.S.A.

Second Edition

Series 500
Audits and Appeals

———————

Tax Guide 505

GOING INTO TAX COURT

For other titles in print, see page 224.

The author: **Holmes F. Crouch**
For more about the author, see page 221.

PREFACE

If you are a knowledge-seeking **taxpayer** looking for information, this book can be helpful to you. It is designed to be read — from cover to cover — in less than eight hours. Or, it can be "skim-read" in about 30 minutes.

Either way, you are treated to **tax knowledge** . . . *beyond the ordinary*. The "beyond" is that which cannot be found in IRS publications, on FedWorld bulletin boards, or from the Web/Internet.

Taxpayers have different levels of interest in a selected subject. For this reason, this book starts with introductory fundamentals and progresses onward. You can verify the progression by chapter and section in the table of contents. In the text, "applicable law" is quoted in pertinent part. Key phrases and key tax forms are emphasized. Real-life examples are given . . . in down-to-earth style.

This book has 12 chapters. This number provides depth without cross-subject rambling. Each chapter starts with a head summary of meaningful information.

To aid in your skim-reading, informative diagrams and tables are placed strategically throughout the text. By leafing through page by page, reading the summaries and section headings, and glancing at the diagrams and tables, you can get a good handle on the matters covered.

Effort has been made to update and incorporate all of the latest tax law changes that are significant to the title subject. However, "beyond the ordinary" does not encompass every conceivable variant of fact and law that might give rise to protracted dispute and litigation. Consequently, if a particular statement or paragraph is crucial to your own specific case, you are urged to seek professional counseling. Otherwise, the information presented is general and is designed for a broad range of reader interests.

The Author

INTRODUCTION

If the Internal Revenue Service (IRS) were an upright and fair-minded bureaucracy, there would be no need for the U.S. Tax Court. As one veteran Tax Court judge said recently: "If the IRS were always right, we'd be out of a job."

The fact that the IRS is not always right is the very reason for Section 7441 of the Internal Revenue Code. This section says—

There is hereby established under Article I of the Constitution of the United States, a court of record to be known as the United States Tax Court.

The mere existence of this statute alone is testimony that the IRS is not a fully trustworthy agency administering the U.S. tax laws. In practice, the IRS is one of the more abusive agencies of government. It has been this way since the Board of Tax Appeals (the predecessor of the Tax Court) was established in 1926.

Because of its long history of abusiveness, the IRS has become THE MOST DISLIKED agency of government. Some of this, of course, is due to the frustration of hard-working taxpayers forking over big bucks to a government that, more often than not, does not spend the money wisely. But much — most — of the ill will is self-inflicted by the IRS. Given the opportunity, it will opt to interpret the tax laws against a taxpayer, then assert maximum penalties under every pretense that it can. It is this practice that generates the widespread distrust of the IRS.

The only balancing lever that a taxpayer has against the IRS is the U.S. Tax Court. It is a weak lever, but it is the only one readily available. If you file a timely petition, your case must be heard.

One of the advantages of Tax Court procedures is that a taxpayer can go into said court on his own. He is not required to be represented by an attorney. This is called "pro se" or "in propria persona": *in one's own person or right.*

Self-representation in Tax Court is advisable when the disputed issues are factual, and the taxpayer has good records and good arguments for his position. It is even advisable when the IRS pyramids its penalties to discourage self-representation. But when a taxpayer is IRS-charged with fraud, failure to file, or other acts bordering on tax evasion, a tax attorney is indeed required.

The problem with the use of attorneys in Tax Court proceedings is that the legal fees often exceed the amount of tax and penalty in dispute. For example, in addressing a tax dispute of $20,000 accompanied by the IRS's assertion of fraud, the attorney fees can quickly exceed $50,000. This is not because the attorney representing the taxpayer wants to drive up his fees — most attorneys dislike the IRS as much as nonattorneys do — it is because the IRS will intentionally drag out the proceedings knowing full well that it can drive up the legal costs higher than the tax and penalty, thereby forcing the taxpayer to concede.

In theory, the Tax Court is supposed to be an unbiased forum for re-examining the IRS's interpretation of a tax law and the applicable facts. But, in practice, it is NOT a level playing field. This is because the Court is more concerned with "protecting revenue" than with protecting taxpayers' pocket books. The Court's attitude is that it is not an advocate for tax justice, nor is it an ombudsman for hearing grievances against the IRS. Its only objective is to determine if — in its opinion — the IRS has made substantial errors in its tax and penalty assessments.

Consequently, the primary goal of this book is to provide those taxpayers who have been mistreated by the IRS — **perhaps you** — with sufficient procedural and tactical knowledge to either go into Tax Court on your own, or with the help of any attorney who will keep his fees reasonable. Our contention is that more taxpayers with bona fide tax and penalty disputes should take advantage of the Tax Court to stand up to the IRS.

As we develop our thesis and goals, we are going to present you with first-hand, in-court experiences of specific real-life tax issues. We will quote actual in-court exchanges between taxpayer, IRS attorney, IRS agents, tax attorney, and Tax Court judge. In these exchanges, you'll be treated to a rare insight into how IRS agents respond under oath. We want you to genuinely "feel" what you are up against, when you get **your** day in Tax Court.

CONTENTS

1

JURISDICTIONAL MATTERS

> The U.S. Tax Court Is A Specialized Tribunal Of "Original Jurisdiction." This Means That All Prior Actions And Abuses By The IRS Are Ignored, And The Amount Of Tax (And Penalties) In Question Start Over "De Novo" (Anew). The Commissioner Of IRS Is The Only Defendant, And There Is No Jury. The Tax Court Is Independent Of The IRS; It Publishes Its Own RULES OF PROCEDURE. Its Authority Is Limited Strictly To Redetermining The Amount Of Federal Tax In Dispute. Although It Can Discipline Taxpayers And Their Attorneys, It Cannot Discipline The IRS.

As its name implies, the United States Tax Court is a court of special jurisdiction. It is "special" in the sense that its legal authority is limited to tax controversies only. It cannot hear any matter other than disputes involving income taxes, gift taxes, death taxes, and certain excise taxes. Its function is to determine the correct tax, under the facts and circumstances presented to it.

The U.S. Tax Court deals only with federal taxes. It cannot hear disputes involving state, county, city, and property taxes. Where there are similarities in tax laws — particularly on matters of income taxes and death taxes — state and local agencies often accept the decisions of the Tax Court as their administrative guide.

The Tax Court is the only court in our entire system of government — federal, state, local — where a tax dispute can be adjudicated *before* payment of the amount in dispute. In all other administrative and judicial processes, one has to pay the tax first, then seek a refund of it (in whole or part).

The Tax Court is a tribunal where a taxpayer has **nearly equal** rights to those of IRS agents who want to overtax and overpenalize him. These rights are not truly equal because the IRS has access to unlimited time, staff, and money — yours and ours — to throw into a tax dispute. Nevertheless, one can probably get a fairer trial in Tax Court than in any other court. This is because the judges assigned are tax specialists rather than generalists in civil and criminal law. Tax Court judges are more concerned with correct tax than maximum revenue. The IRS is more concerned with maximum revenue . . . and maximum penalties.

In this chapter, therefore, we want to preview the general jurisdictional aspects of Tax Court proceedings. We want to point out what you can and cannot do. We also want to point out what the court itself can and cannot do. We'll defer until later chapters to tell you what the IRS can do, does do, and cannot do.

The Constitutional Origin

The Constitution of the U.S. consists of a preamble, eight articles of enactment, 10 rights contained in a "Bill," and 16 amendments. The first three enacting articles are called the "powers articles." They delineate the power of government into three separate branches, namely: legislative, executive, and judicial.

The leadoff sentence in each of the three powers articles is:

Article I. All legislative powers herein shall be vested in a Congress of the United States, which shall consist of a Senate and House of Representatives.

Article II. The executive power shall be vested in a President of the United States.

Article III. The judicial power of the United States shall be vested in one Supreme Court, and in such inferior courts as the Congress may from time to time ordain and establish.

The Tax Court is constitutionalized under Article I: **not** under Article III as one might suspect. This is because it is a specialized court established by Congress to oversee the revenue collection laws of government. This legislative establishment evolves from Section 8 of Article I which says—

The Congress shall have the power to lay and collect taxes, duties, imposts and excises ... [which] *shall be uniform throughout the United States.*

The net effect of Article I is that the U.S. Tax Court is created as an independent tribunal of its own. It is not empowered to hear general law matters as is the case with other federal courts constituted under Article III.

Because the word "tax" appears in its name, many taxpayers assume that the Tax Court is an enforcement arm of the IRS. This is **not** the arrangement. The Tax Court is an entirely independent agency of its own. It is a legislative-judicial entity which can — and often does — render decisions against the IRS.

A representation of the independence of the Tax Court from the IRS is presented in Figure 1.1. The IRS cannot ignore the decisions of the Tax Court, though it can contest those decisions into higher courts. So, too, can a taxpayer contest the decision of the Tax Court.

A One Defendant Court

The Tax Court has several unique characteristics which distinguish it from all other judicial forms. One of these characteristics is that there is always the same defendant. That defendant is the IRS. No other person or entity can be a defendant in Tax Court.

Ordinarily, a defendant is any person or entity against whom legal action is sought. But in Tax Court matters, there is always the same defendant. For reasons which will be more clear later, the term *respondent* is used rather than defendant.

The only respondent in a Tax Court case is the Commissioner of Internal Revenue. The IRS Commissioner is an appointee of the President. This fact should be self-evident in Figure 1.1. The Commissioner himself, of course, never responds. He has a whole battery of attorneys — paid for by taxpayers — who respond in his behalf. Nevertheless, every petition to the Tax Court must name the Commissioner of Internal Revenue as the respondent.

There are in excess of 130,000,000 (130 million) persons and entities in the United States who file federal tax returns annually, in

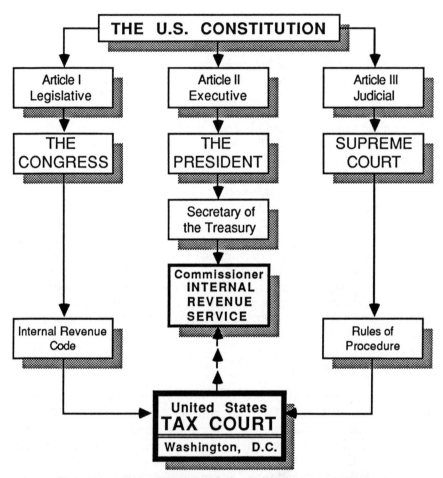

Fig. 1.1 - U.S. Tax Court: An Independent Tribunal

one form or another. Any one of these 130 million taxpayers can file a petition in Tax Court for redress of a dispute with the IRS. The reverse is not true, however.

The IRS cannot petition the Tax Court against a taxpayer. That is, it cannot be a plaintiff/petitioner in said court. It doesn't need to. Administratively, the IRS has almost totalitarian powers of levy and seizure against those persons and entities who do not exercise their rights in Tax Court. The IRS can be — and often is — plaintiff/petitioner in other federal courts, but not in Tax Court.

Tax Court procedures, therefore, are a very special right allowed to taxpayers only. The IRS is not a tax *paying* entity by any stretch of imagination.

Not a Jury Court

There is another special feature which sets the Tax Court apart from other court forms. It is not a jury court. That is, a taxpayer cannot be heard before a jury of his peers. There are several reasons for this.

One reason is that the Tax Court has to focus on the fine points of tax law. To do this effectively, the court must allow all reasonably relevant facts and circumstances to be presented. The proper relevancy and interpretation of these facts often are too highly technical for comprehension by ordinary jurors. In very complex tax cases, more than one Tax Court judge is co-assigned. Thus, the effect of a jury of multiple minds is preserved, though no ordinary jury is involved.

The second reason for no jury is that the same defendant — the IRS — appears over and over again. An agency which has such devastating powers as the IRS would invariably intimidate a jury. So, even if a jury trial were allowed, jurors would be afraid to render a decision against the IRS.

The third, and perhaps most important, reason why no jury is allowed is because no truly impartial jury could be found. Every productive person in the United States, at one time or another, has had some nasty experience with the IRS. It would be difficult to find a group of jurors who could be completely neutral towards the IRS. Consequently, anyone on a jury would, if given a chance, almost certainly decide against the IRS. Yet, the IRS is not always wrong. There are many vexatious tax protesters around who want to be no part of the U.S. tax system.

A good-faith tax disputant actually has an advantage in Tax Court without a jury. The nitty-gritty of the tax issue can be gotten into more quickly. Because of their specialized jurisdiction, Tax Court judges are more knowledgeable in their field, and generally are more tolerant towards taxpayers than other court judges.

Entombed in Tax Code

Congress makes all of the tax laws . . . too many of them. There are approximately 1,800 separate tax laws, not counting the thousands of subsections and sub-subsections thereto. They comprise nearly 9,000 pages of text, including amendments and annotations. They are published in a special document called: THE INTERNAL REVENUE CODE. Every year, new laws are added and a few old ones are repealed.

The IR Code is officially designated as Title 26: United States Code. This body of tax commands is organized into subtitles, chapters, subchapters, and sections. For thumbnail overview purposes, a highly abbreviated outline of the IR Code is presented in Figure 1.2. There you will note that we have expanded slightly on Subtitle F: Procedure and Administration.

Within Subtitle F, there is a separate Subchapter C headed: **The Tax Court**. The leadoff section therein reads—

Sec. 7441 — There is hereby established, under article I of the Constitution of the United States, a court of record to be known as the United States Tax Court. The members of the Tax Court shall be the chief judge and the judges of the Tax Court.

This is the only court established by direct enactment in the revenue laws. It is therefore "entombed" therein. Other federal courts are established by other Acts of Congress.

Other establishing features found in the IR Code are:

Sec. 7442 — The Tax Court and its divisions shall have such jurisdiction as is conferred on them by this title [Title 26: U.S. Code, Internal Revenue].

Sec. 7443 — The Tax Court shall be composed of 19 members. Judges of the Tax Court shall be appointed by the President, by and with the advice and consent of the Senate, solely on the grounds of fitness to perform the duties of the office.

Sec. 7443A — The chief judge may, from time to time, appoint special trial judges who shall proceed under such rules and regulations as may be promulgated by the Tax Court.

Sec. 7444 — The Tax Court shall have a seal which shall be judicially noticed.

TITLE 26: U.S.CODE - INTERNAL REVENUE

Subtitle A - **INCOME TAXES**
Chapters 1 to 10; Sections 1 to 1564

Subtitle B - **ESTATE & GIFT TAXES**
Chapters 11 to 20; Sections 2001 to 2704

Subtitle C - **EMPLOYMENT TAXES**
Chapters 21 to 30; Sections 3101 to 3510

Subtitle D - **EXCISE TAXES**
Chapters 31 to 50; Sections 4001 to 5000

Subtitle E - **ALCOHOL, TOBACCO TAXES**
Chapters 51 to 60; Sections 5001 to 5880

Subtitle F - **PROCEDURE & ADMINISTRATION**
Chapters 61 to 90; Sections 6001 to 7874

Chapter 76: JUDICIAL PROCEEDINGS
Subchapter A - Civil Actions by IRS
Subchapter B - Proceedings by Taxpayers

Subchapter C - THE TAX COURT
Sections 7441 to 7478

Subchapter D - Review of Tax Court Decisions
Sections 7481 to 7487

Subtitle G - **JOINT COMMITTEE ON TAXATION**
Chapters 91 to 92; Sections 8001 to 8024

Subtitle H - **FINANCING PRESIDENTIAL ELECTIONS**
Chapters 95 to 96; Sections 9001 to 9042

Subtitle I - **TRUST FUND CODE**
Chapter 98; Sections 9501 to 9602

Subtitle J - **COAL INDUSTRY HEALTH BENEFITS**
Chapter 99; Sections 9701 to 9722

Fig. 1.2 - Highly Abbreviated Outline of Internal Revenue Code

Sec. 7445 — The principal office of the Tax Court shall be in the District of Columbia, but the Tax Court or any of its divisions may sit at any place within the United States.

It is not our intention here to recite the approximately 30 sections of the tax code which set forth the organization and functions of the Tax Court. We simply want you to be aware that said court has ample authority to **redetermine** the tax allegations of the IRS. The guiding source for both the IRS and the Tax Court is the IR Code.

Having a common reference source for two government agencies means that there can be two official interpretations of the same tax dispute. The IRS interpretation is administrative; the Tax Court interpretation is judicial. If a dispute goes on from this point, the decision of the Tax Court is the one which is judicially noticed. This is what is meant by *a court of record.*

Simple Organizational Structure

Because no jury is involved, and because only tax disputes are considered, the organizational structure of the Tax Court is quite simple. There is only one principal office, that in Washington, D.C. This location is a practical convenience; the national office of the IRS Commissioner also is located in Washington, D.C.

Having its principal office in Washington, D.C. does not mean that all tax cases are heard there. The actual hearings are held in approximately 65 cities throughout the United States. The "local offices" are in federal buildings in designated cities. Said offices (and court rooms) are not regularly staffed. They are staffed only when the Tax Court is in session, which depends on the frequency of tax disputes in that area. In major metropolitan centers, tax disputes are sufficiently frequent that local sessions are held on a regular calendar basis.

There are 19 Tax Court judges and (currently) 11 special trial judges. One is the Chief Judge. Five judges are assigned to administrative duties to review all Tax Court petitions and decisions. These five are called Division Judges. They remain in Washington, D.C.

All others are designated as Circuit Judges. That is, each Circuit Judge hears cases in approximately five or six different cities as needed. Each such judge travels from city to city throughout the year, instead of remaining sequestered in judicial chambers. This mellows them a bit, and puts them more in touch with taxpayer reality. But don't take too much stock in this. As government employees, all Tax Court judges are a "protected species." Very few have faced the hard knocks of the business world. Probably none has ever faced the computer wrath and disreputable behavior of the IRS as an ordinary citizen.

Though it moves around from city to city, there is only one official mailing address of the Tax Court. That address is—

**United States Tax Court
400 Second Street, N.W.
Washington, D.C. 20217**

We want you to implant this one address firmly in your mind. This is where you send all of your original Tax Court papers. You do not send the originals to the IRS.

All Tax Court judges are appointed by the President for a term of 15 years. Each judge is eligible for reappointment to successive terms. This length of tenure enables them to develop a high degree of technical expertise in tax matters. Although the President also appoints the Commissioner of Internal Revenue, the IRS Commissioner's maximum term of office is four to eight years. Some presidents have appointed two and three IRS Commissioners during their presidential terms. Hence, Tax Court judges are less apt to be affected by changing political tides, as are IRS Commissioners.

TC Rules of Procedure

The Tax Court operates as a court of original jurisdiction. This means that all documents, evidence, and procedures for the hearing of a tax dispute start all over from the beginning. All of those computer demands and threats that the IRS has sent you over the course of your dispute are tossed aside. This is the theory of "original jurisdiction." In practice, however, the IRS simply reprints its morass of computer assertions and reheads them as the TC (Tax Court) respondent.

Altogether there are about 160 rules and 16 official forms promulgated by the Tax Court for procedural purposes. These TC rules and forms are set forth in a clear and explicit manner in approximately 200 pages of text. This is a rare treat for taxpayers who want to protect their rights without having to wade through a forest of legalese. Anyone who can read can understand the Tax Court rules. This cannot be said for those rules published by other federal courts.

An abbreviated outline of the TC rules and appendices is presented in Figure 1.3. Note that what ordinarily might be classed as a chapter is called a "title" in court jargon. This is a carryover from medieval days when only persons of title could enter a court. Otherwise, the heavy hand of obfuscation and fine-point legality is nowhere as objectionable in the TC rules as in the IR Code.

The Tax Court is a more down-to-earth judicial body. Extreme formality is not its forte. A few random citations from its rules will illustrate what we mean. For example, Rule 1(b) says—

These Rules shall be construed to secure the just, speedy, and inexpensive determination of every case.

Why doesn't the IRS obey this "speedy and inexpensive" rule? When you get through this book, you'll know why. The IRS obeys a different drummer, called: "powers of extraconstitutionality."

Going further, TC Rule 23(c) says—

Papers filed with the Court may be prepared by any process, but only if all papers, including copies, filed with the Court are clear and legible.

And Rule 31(a) says—

The purpose of the pleadings is to give the parties and the Court fair notice of the matters in controversy and the basis for their respective positions.

Wait until you read (several chapters later) how the IRS "pleads" — mandates — its position(s) in a controversy. You'll probably conclude that the IRS can't — or won't — read the TC rules.

By these selected citations, we simply want to point out that the Tax Court rules can be comprehended by any person of ordinary intelligence. Furthermore, the rules are not computer printed and hackneyed like most IRS communications. The TC rules are printed "the old-fashioned way": with capital letters, lower cases, bold print, italics, variable type font, with sufficient white space such that each heading, subheading, and paragraph stands on its own. Anyone can get a copy of the TC rules by writing to the Clerk of the Court, at the Tax Court address previously given.

RULES OF PRACTICE & PROCEDURE
U.S. TAX COURT

TITLE	CONTENTS	RULES
I.	Scope & Definitions	1 to 3
II.	Court & Jurisdiction	10 to 13
III.	Commencement & Appearance	20 to 25
IV.	Pleadings & Answers	30 to 41
V.	Motions & Dispositions	50 to 58
VI.	Parties & Substitutes	60 to 63
VII.	Discovery & Interrogatories	70 to 76
VIII.	Depositions & Objections	80 to 85
IX.	Admissions & Stipulations	90 to 92
X.	Provisions re Discovery	100 to 104
XI.	Pretrial Conferences	110
XII.	Decision Without Trial	120 to 124
XIII.	Calendars & Continuances	130 to 134
XIV.	Trials & Evidence	140 to 152
XV.	Entry of Decision	155 to 157
XVI.	Post-Trial Proceedings	160 to 163
XVII.	Small Tax Cases	170 to 179
XVIII.	Special Trial Judges	180 to 183
XIX.	Appeals & Bonds	190 to 193
XX.	Practice Before the Court	200 to 202
XXI.	Declaratory Judgments	210 to 218
XXII.	Disclosure Actions	220 to 229
XXIII.	Claims for Costs	230 to 233
XXIV.	Partnership Actions	240 to 251
XXV.	Supplemental Proceedings	260 to 262
XXVI.	Actions for Admin. Costs	270 to 274

Appendix I.   Petition & Subpoena Forms
Appendix II.   Disputes of $10,000 or Less
Appendix III. Fees & Charges
Appendix IV.   Places of Trial

INDEX

Fig. 1.3 - Abbreviated Outline of Tax Court Rules

Decisions Rendered: Not Judgments

The Tax Court renders decisions; it does not render judgments. There is a distinction here.

A judgment is a court order (command) which can be enforced by the court itself. Enforcement is by fine, seizure, restraint, and/or imprisonment. Unlike other federal courts, the Tax Court is not empowered to enforce its own decisions. This is *not* a shortcoming; it is a manifestation of the structural wisdom of Tax Court proceedings.

Think about the situation for a moment. The only defendant/respondent is the Commissioner of Internal Revenue. He is an appointee of the President. The Tax Court judge is also an appointee of the President. Think of the political fireworks and embarrassment to the President if a tax decision were rendered against the IRS, and the Tax Court judge sought enforcement by imprisoning the IRS Commissioner!

But politics is not the reason why enforcement powers are not given to the Tax Court. The tax decisions are self-enforcing. Let us explain.

If the Tax Court rules against the IRS, and the IRS Commissioner does not appeal to a higher court, the IRS simply cannot collect the tax that it alleges is due. In other words, the IRS is deprived of its collection authority — on the disputed amount — if it loses in Tax Court.

On the other hand, if a taxpayer/petitioner loses in Tax Court, what happens? The IRS collects the tax (period).

The IRS has ample authority to collect any tax on its own, without judicial enforcement. In most cases, all the IRS has to do is to mail NOTICE AND DEMAND for payment. Most taxpayers will pay on IRS demand, but, for those who do not, the IRS has levy and seizure powers. It first levies and seizes your bank accounts. If your bank accounts have insufficient funds, the IRS will then levy and seize your wages and salaries. If you are unemployed or self-employed, the IRS sends a tow truck and hauls away all vehicles, machinery, and equipment on, or adjacent to, your premises. It sells these items at public auction for 10 cents on the fair-market dollar. If the collected proceeds are not enough, the IRS then records a federal tax lien on all real property in your name. It deliberately doubles and triples the liened amount (by pyramiding penalties) so that when the property is regularly sold, there is no money left for you, the taxpayer. Hence, obviously, the IRS needs no enforcement help whatsoever from the Tax Court.

Cannot Discipline the IRS

The one glaring weakness of the Tax Court is that it cannot discipline the IRS. It can discipline taxpayers and/or their attorneys, but not the IRS. Congress won't discipline the IRS, and the President won't either. This leaves the taxpayer out on a limb for addressing any misdeeds of the IRS that led up to the tax dispute. One's only consolation is that, once a dispute is in Tax Court, the IRS will at least suspend its abusiveness while in the direct presence of the Tax Court judge.

In the IR Code, there are some 55 different penalties that the IRS can, does, and will assert and levy against the taxpayer. In the same IR Code, **not a single penalty can be asserted against the IRS by a taxpayer.** This situation needs to be corrected; we offer corrective suggestions in Chapter 12.

The point we are making is that if there is no provision in the IR Code for a penalty assertion against the IRS, going into Tax Court offers no forum for addressing the vexatious behavior of the IRS.

There is, however, one disciplinary section in the IR Code which the Tax Court is authorized to administer. This is **Section 6673**: Sanctions and Costs Awarded by Courts. Subsection 6673(a)(1) addresses the Tax Court Proceedings as follows:

> *Whenever it appears to the Tax Court that—*
> *(A) proceedings before it have been instituted or maintained **by the taxpayer** primarily for delay,*
> *(B) the **taxpayer's position** in such proceeding is frivolous or groundless, or*
> *(C) the **taxpayer unreasonably failed** to pursue available administrative remedies,*
> *the Tax Court, in it decision, may require the taxpayer to pay to the United States a penalty not in excess of $25,000.* [Emphasis added.]

Section 6673(a) applies to all TC proceedings instituted after October 22, 1986. The central message here is that when you do go into Tax Court, all responsibility is upon you to proceed in good faith with a bona fide tax dispute. You probably would not go into said court otherwise.

As for any remote disciplinary action against the IRS, the IR Code addresses only those IRS attorneys who appear in Tax Court. On this point, subsection 6673(a)(2): Counsel's Liability for Excessive Costs, says—

Whenever it appears to the Tax Court that any attorney . . . has multiplied the proceedings . . . unreasonably and vexatiously, the Tax Court may require—
(B) if such attorney is appearing on behalf of the Commissioner of Internal Revenue, that the United States pay such excess costs, expenses, and attorneys' fees in the same manner as such an award by a district court.

This latter tax code wording is a round robin and dead end. The Tax Court has never issued an "excess costs award" against an IRS attorney. And, even if it were ever to do so, the awarded taxpayer would have to file an entirely separate legal action in a U.S. District Court. The collection action would have to name the United States as the defendant, and not the Commissioner of Internal Revenue. The net result is that any disciplinary effect on the IRS by subsection 6673(a)(2)(B) is nil.

TC Records Are Public

Except for unusual cases involving financial privacy, trade secrets, and competitive confidentiality, all Tax court records are available to the public. That is, of course, after a decision has been reached and timely entered into official records.

The post-decision access to Tax Court records is a matter of public policy. Said policy is set forth in Section 7461(a) of the IR Code, as follows:

Except as provided in subsection (b) [re trade secrets or other confidential information], *all reports of the Tax Court and all evidence received by the Tax Court and its divisions, including a transcript of the stenographic report of the hearings, shall be public records open to the inspection of the public.*

Echoing the same sentiment, TC Rule 12(b) says—

After the Court renders its decision in a case, a plain or certified copy of any document, record, entry, or other paper, pertaining to the case and still in custody of the Court, may be obtained upon application to the Court's Copywork Office and payment of the required fee.

Our suggestion is that, if you are going to get serious about pursuing a matter in Tax Court, you first write to the Clerk of the Court for a copy of its Rules of Practice and Procedure. Use the address that we gave you earlier on page 1-9. Include a check for $9 (current cost) payable to U.S. Tax Court. Allow approximately two weeks for the mailing.

It is important that you have a copy of the TC Rules in your hands. On the inside front cover is a listing of the different offices of the clerical organization of the court. Each of the offices is identified by function and phone number. A phone call is the quickest way to get your nonlegal questions answered and to expedite the receipt of identifiable information, papers, or forms that you may want.

All Tax Court cases start with a taxpayer's petition. As the petitions are received by the Clerk, each is assigned a **Docket No.** This number is stamped on all papers thereafter filed in the case, and is the reference locator for all correspondence therewith. The Docket No. is consecutively assigned, followed by the year in which the petition is received. For example, Docket No. 28098-95 would be the 28,098th petition received by the court in 1995.

Incidentally, the Tax Court receives close to 30,000 taxpayer petitions each year. Consequently, you are not alone, if you have a bona fide tax dispute.

Self-Representation is Proper

One of the appealing features of Tax Court proceedings is that self-representation is accepted. It is accepted as one's right to do his own tax return and proceed on his own through any and all phases of IRS audit and appeal. A taxpayer generally knows his own tax affairs better than anyone else. He may — and probably does — lack knowledge on the technical fine points of tax law. If one is not completely sure about his position, he can always seek professional tax advice and guidance along the way. He does not absolutely need an attorney.

Self-representation is not openly encouraged by the Tax Court, but it is not covertly discouraged either. TC **Rule 24(b)** makes this point quite clear. Said rule is titled: **Personal Representation Without Counsel**. It says—

> *In the absence of appearance by counsel, a party will be deemed to appear on the party's own behalf. An individual party may represent himself or herself. . . . Any such person shall state, in the initial pleading or other paper filed by or for the party, such person's name, address, and telephone number, and thereafter shall promptly notify the Clerk in writing, in duplicate for each docket number involving that party, of any change in that information.*

Obviously, one should use common sense and prudence when representing himself. If the dispute involves the IRS's allegation of fraud or willful tax evasion, a qualified attorney (admitted to practice before the Tax Court) is a "must." If the IRS has asserted "substantial omission of income" (meaning more than 25% unreported), qualified counsel should be employed. Thus, if you feel the need for an attorney, be sure that he/she is a *tax* attorney. An ordinary attorney will not do. The reason for a tax attorney is that you will be dealing with extraconstitutional powers and behavior of the IRS, which violates the legal training tenets of ordinary attorneys.

Before deciding to go on your own, take a realistic assessment of yourself. Do you have the self-discipline and perseverance — and the stomach for an adversarial enemy — to stick it out? Are you temperamentally prepared for delays and continuances by the IRS? Do you have keenness of insight for spotting the dirty tricks that IRS attorneys, agents, and officials will employ to catch you off guard and confuse you? Once trial begins, don't expect any help, other than nominal procedural guidance, from the Tax Court judge. Otherwise, IRS attorneys will jump all over the judge and move that your case be dismissed. Dismissal means that you lose. Then the IRS collection agents will be on your trail immediately.

2

EXAMPLES OF DISPUTES

The Most Important Prerequisites For Tax Court Are That You: (1) File A Return, (2) Endure An Audit, And (3) Seek Appeal Within The IRS. These Steps Enable A Dispute To Be Better Formulated Into The Core Issue(s). The IRS Drags Its Feet Knowing Full Well That The Daily Compounding Of Interest On Its Asserted Deficiency And Penalties Will Put Pressure On You. By Alleging Fraud, The IRS Can Audit 6 Consecutive Years Of Returns. There Is No Better Way Of Understanding The Pre-Tax Court Process Than By Citing SPECIFIC EXAMPLES Of Bona Fide Taxpayer Disputes.

Entry into Tax Court requires first of all that you have a bona fide tax dispute. That is, the dispute must be based on some item on your tax return, with which you have taken a good faith position in some variant interpretation of existing tax law. Going in on moral grounds, political grounds, or convictions of the "unfairness" of the tax laws will get you nowhere. After all, it was your Congress that enacted the laws, and your President who signed them. The presumption is that these elected persons knew what they were doing . . . or should have known.

Nor can you question the legitimacy and behavior of the IRS. It is an extraconstitutional arm of Congress and the President with a job to do. That job, simply, is to assess a tax upon you (called: "collection of revenue") and direct it into the U.S. Treasury where

Congress and the President can spend your money. If you have difficulty with this, the Tax Court is not your forum.

Where the Tax Court is your forum is where the IRS has twisted the tax laws against you in its drive for maximum revenue. If you are alert to this behavior and can identify the IRS's twisting, you have the seed beginnings of a bona fide dispute.

In this chapter, we want to present the prerequisites for a bona fide tax dispute, and give some examples of how these disputes originate. Not all disputes wind up in Tax Court. Most taxpayers simply give in to the IRS. If you don't give in, and want to proceed into Tax Court, you must do so with each of your disputive issues well formulated. Even then, the IRS will put roadblocks in your way at every step.

Return(s) Must Be Filed

A tax dispute, by definition, must originate from a federal tax return . . . any return. Whether a return is filed on time, filed upon extension, or filed late, is not the issue. There has to be some item on, or omission from, the return that affects the collection of maximum revenue by the IRS. Remember, it is money, money, money that the IRS is after. It can't determine the correct amount of money, without your filing the appropriate tax return.

Oh, yes. There are legitimate occasions for which no tax return is required, or, where required, no tax is due. But this doesn't stop the IRS from levying upon your bank account(s).

A recent true case will illustrate this point.

The taxpayer was a merchant mariner on a tug boat servicing multiple oil-drilling platforms in the Persian Gulf. He worked in the Persian Gulf for nearly three years. He was paid by a U.S. Company out of its home office in Texas. His compensation ranged between $35,000 and $50,000 each year, not including meals and quarters, which were furnished by the employer. He was informed by his U.S. employer that his foreign duty pay was eligible for the $70,000 annual exclusion authorized by Section 911(b)(2)(A) of the IR Code. So, he filed no tax returns for each of the three years he was overseas. Guess what happened?

Under its authority of Section 6020(b), the IRS fabricated a tax return for each of the missing years based on information supplied to it by the taxpayer's employer. Using its routine tactic of "pyramiding all penalties," the IRS assessed a tax of approximately $27,000 for each of the missing return years. It then levied and seized all of the taxpayer's bank accounts in the U.S., and levied and seized all subsequent wages of the taxpayer until the total asserted amount of money was taken.

This particular victim has no basis for a Tax Court petition. He didn't file any tax returns on his own. Had he filed a return for each of his foreign duty years, and had he claimed the $70,000 exclusion for each of those years, he would have had no tax to pay. Had he filed his returns timely, and had the IRS then seized his money, he would have had a very legitimate dispute for Tax Court ears.

IRS Computer Errors

The IRS is so overcomputerized these days that even when you file a return accurately, computer generated disputes can emerge. With total reliance on the infallibility of its computers, IRS personnel rarely eye-ball a return any more. Information on a return is computer scanned and transcribed by electronic readers of line numbers only. Any insertions or explanations on the preprinted form lines are ignored. The result is that taxpayers are inundated with computer demands for more taxes, even when no additional tax is due.

Take the recent case of a dentist in private practice, for example. He had invested $85,000 into a new prophylactic device for the treatment of gum disease on back teeth. The device was modestly successful, but the company developing it filed for bankruptcy. The dentist filed a protective claim with the bankruptcy referee, and eventually was refunded $50,000 of his investment. The referee computer reported to the IRS the $50,000 as "nonemployee compensation" (on Form 1099-MISC).

Anything reported to the IRS as "nonemployee compensation" has got to show up on Schedule C (Form 1040): Profit or Loss from Business. There it is subject to *two* taxes: income tax and social security tax. Since the dentist had customarily reported his income and expenses on Schedule C, he prepared a second Schedule C reporting his investment refund. He negated out the $50,000 so as to show zero on the bottom line. At the negation-out line, he entered this notation (in hand-printed bold red letters):

Erroneously Reported by Payer;
See Schedule D (Form 1040)

Simultaneously, he prepared a Schedule D (Capital Gains and Losses) and attached it to his return. Properly, he entered his initial investment as $85,000 and the $50,000 refund as "sales proceeds." The net effect was that he was entitled to a $35,000 capital *loss*.

Nevertheless, the IRS computer demanded income tax, social security tax, penalties, and interest on the $50,000.

This is the case of a bona fide tax dispute. However, the unwritten procedure is that when the IRS makes an error, the burden is on the taxpayer to notify the IRS of its error. You can't go into Tax Court unless you can show that you've done this.

Must "Go Through" Audit

The IRS has authority, under IR Code Section 7602: Examination of Books and Witnesses, to examine any return, any time, for any reason. It does not have to explain the reason, other than its authority for doing so. Usually, but not always, it will indicate vaguely those items or groups of items on which it will initially focus.

Even though you know that your return is absolutely correct, and you have the documents to prove it, you cannot avoid an audit examination when so notified. Don't even hint at wanting to do so. You are expected to "cooperate" docilely. If you fail to cooperate, that fact will be glaringly boomed against you in Tax Court.

When the IRS demands that you "cooperate" at an audit, it is a one-way affair. To illustrate this, we cite a case where the audit turned up additional deductions allowable on Schedule A (Form 1040) beyond those originally entered.

The taxpayer (a socialite divorcee) entered $65,000 on Schedule A (Itemized Deductions) as legal and accounting expenses in connection with a $4,000,000 ($4 million) property settlement. Before looking at the cancelled checks and invoices, the auditor painstakingly went through the property settlement papers: about 35 pages. The auditor concluded that she would allow the taxpayer 76% of all legal and accounting expenses for the income-producing property that the taxpayer was to receive.

When the auditor totaled the verified expenses, the amount came to $103,000. Upon applying the 76% allowability fraction, the allowable entry would have been $78,000 instead of the $65,000 on the return. Suddenly, the auditor changed her mind. She said (as paraphrased):

"I'm only going to allow 63% of your $103,000 legal and accounting expenses. This comes out to the $65,000 as initially entered on your return."

This would have been a great disputational issue before the Tax Court. The IRS refused to compute the correct tax which happened to be *lower* than the amount of tax paid with the return.

In this particular case, the taxpayer, already stressed out from the divorce entanglements, accepted the auditor's "no change" proposal. Once an unfavorable position is accepted by a taxpayer, he (she) cannot later change his (her) mind to institute Tax Court proceedings. The IRS can change its mind, but not a taxpayer.

Must Timely Appeal

It is an established IRS procedure that, if you receive an adverse *Report of Examination Change* after an audit, you must appeal that report (within the IRS) or accept the consequences. You have 30 days to notify the IRS of your intention, one way or the other. By far the great majority of audit reports are adverse to taxpayers. As revealed above, audits are not performed to refund money.

The audit appeals process is an internal administrative process conducted solely by the IRS. The disputed tax and/or penalty is turned over to new eyes and ears in an Appeals Division. In most cases, the process is perfunctory and time consuming. Rarely are any significant changes made to the audit reports. In small tax matters only, sometimes favorable changes are made. But, by and large, appeals officers don't want to be criticized by their IRS superiors for reducing the audit ante for maximum revenue. As a result, the IRS appeals process more often serves as a "cooling off" period for sapping the vitality of taxpayer disputes.

Here's a good illustration of the sapping effect of the administrative appeals offer.

A taxpayer and spouse retired to a new location after suffering earthquake damage to their former home. They conscientiously and cooperatively went through the audit process. They provided the auditor with voluminous photographs of the earthquake damage. They prepared Form 4684: Casualties and Thefts, and headnoted it: "Disaster Loss: 7.1 Earthquake: 10-17-89." They entered the amount of damage based on preliminary estimates over the phone by appraisers who were too busy on other more devastated properties.

The auditor, some 18 months after the quake, insisted that the taxpayers get a written appraisal of the damage. During that 18-month period, the taxpayers had cleared up the debris and made some of the repairs themselves. Naturally, the written appraisal was less than the original estimate. Thereupon, the auditor assigned them an additional tax of $2,790. That was bad enough. The auditor also arbitrarily assigned them the 20% accuracy-related penalty [Sec. 6662(c)] for—

Negligence and intentional disregard of rules and regulations.

The audit report showed $2,790 in additional tax plus $558 penalty. We think the audit report was wrong and that the negligence penalty was unconscionable. But is $3,348 (2,790 + 558) worth going through the motions of appeal, waiting months and months for no corrective action, then spending more months to get the matter into Tax Court?

The average tax and penalty that an IRS audit produces is approximately $3,500 per individual return per year. If the amount in dispute is less than this average, the IRS and the Tax Court will not treat the matter seriously.

Limit IRS's Drag Time

Whether the amount of tax (and penalty) in dispute is $1,000 or $30,000, one must still go through the IRS appeals process before the way is cleared for Tax Court. But this doesn't mean that you must let the IRS tie your hands by dragging its feet. The greater the amount in dispute, the greater the foot dragging that goes on. IRS appeals officers constitute a pool of aspirants to upper management in the bureaucracy. They are not going to make any decisions beneficial to taxpayers that will jeopardize their promotions.

Think about the appeals situation for a moment. Suppose you had a bona fide dispute somewhere between $30,000 and $50,000. Once in Tax Court, disputes of this magnitude are seldom all winners or all losers. The typical odds are 50/50. You may win 50% of your dispute, and the IRS may win 50%. IRS appeals officers know this. They also know that the dollar magnitude in dispute is on a par with their annual salary range. Are they going to rule $20,000 to $25,000 in your favor, which is half of their annual salary? If they were to do so, do you think they would get promoted?

The reality is that for substantial tax disputes — those exceeding $10,000 per taxable year — IRS appeals personnel are simply going to drag their feet. They keep dragging until six months prior to the statute of limitations. Normally, the IRS has three years after the due date of a return to assess additional tax against you [IRC Sec. 6501(a)]. So, at the six-month mark, the appeals officer will send you a filled-in **Form 872-A**: Special Consent to Extend Time to Assess Tax. You'll be asked to sign it. By signing it, you extend the three-year statutory time indefinitely. Our advice is: DON'T SIGN IT!

By not signing the Form 872-A waiver, the appeals officer will then issue a statutory Notice of Deficiency. This will clear the way for you to petition directly to the Tax Court. You **have** to go through the audit process and appeals process first. These are the prerequisites to a "tax dispute" which we summarize in Figure 2.1.

> *Editorial Note*: In various paragraphs below, we'll recite four specific tax disputes. We'll carry these examples through subsequent chapters so that you'll see exactly how they are handled in real-life Tax Court proceedings. We need at least this number of examples in order to bring out the variant practices of the IRS and the Tax Court. We'll tell you right off that all four examples are the first-hand experiences of the author herein. Since this book is about going INTO Tax Court, the author felt it essential that he experience the process himself.

Specific Dispute I

In 1981, the author — a tax return preparer — heard on national TV a presidential proclamation declaring May 1981 as "Older Americans Month." The proclamation was a public appeal to help *enhance the lives of older Americans.* No specific suggestions were made as to how this could be done. The proclamation, however, was concurrent with the then-pending "bankruptcy of the Social Security system." We hear these same bankruptcy words today.

The author was age 62 at the time, and could have stopped work and begun to collect his own Social Security benefits for the rest of his life. He thought the matter over for several days, then asked himself:

"Why not make a public gift of my lifelong Social Security benefits for those senior citizens in greater need than I? As a self-employed tax preparer, I can work as long as I am

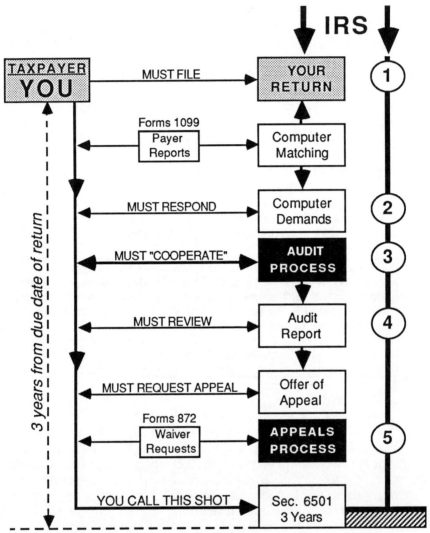

Fig. 2.1 - The Prerequisites of a Bona Fide Tax Dispute

physically able to, without having to depend on Social Security
. . . ever."

The author talked it over with his wife. She thought it was a
good idea. He phoned his Congressman's office and talked it over

with his administrative assistant. She, too, thought it was a good idea and that the Congressman would be genuinely pleased.

The author visited the local office of the Social Security Administration and mentioned the idea to various interviewers there. The paraphrased response was—

"We've never heard of anyone doing that before. We have no procedures for accepting such a gift. All we can do is give you an estimate of your initial lifetime monthly benefits."

Based on these reactions, the author on May 12, 1981 had his wife type a letter to the President. It was the President who signed the "Older Americans Month" Proclamation on April 29, 1981. In said letter, the author renounced his lifetime Social Security benefits as a public gift for those in greater need. He had the letter notarized and sent a copy to his Congressman. He requested his Congressman to also send a copy to the Social Security Administration for recording there. On June 23, 1981, the Congressman sent a return letter to the author saying—

The action you have taken is a generous one, deserving the gratitude of other, less fortunate Americans.

Being a tax preparer, the author was not going to give up his lifetime Social Security benefits without taking advantage of a charitable deduction on Schedule A (Form 1040): Itemized Deductions. Accordingly, on his 1981 Schedule A: Contributions, the author entered the following information:

Sec. 170(c)(1)	*$88,583*
Soc. Sec. Entitlement (62)	
170(b)(1)(A)(v): 50% AGI	
Carryover to 1982	*<73,936>*

He filed his completed 1981 return in January 1982. He attached a copy of his letter to the President, and a copy of the letter from his Congressman, to the return.

Upon proper notification, the IRS auditor visited the taxpayer's premises in June, 1984 to conduct her examination of the 1981 return. It was immediately obvious that she had the charitable deduction entry in mind. Without asking for any background information, she said (as paraphrased):

"We think you're trying to get away with something. I'm here to warn you that you are not going to. We're going to audit your returns for the next 5 years. And we're going to assess all the penalties against you that we can think of."

She then asked the author how he arrived at the $88,583 figure. He showed the auditor the official estimate of his Social Security benefits ($439 per month) and the actuarial life expectancy tables which the taxpayer's Congressman had received from the Social Security Administration. The computation checked out perfectly ($439/mo x 12 mo/yr x 16.8 yrs = $88,583).

It didn't matter. The auditor's mind was made up. She disallowed the entire amount and set in motion her justification for imposing maximum penalties. Without giving you more details at this point, we will identify this dispute as: ISSUE I - Public Gift.

Specific Dispute II

In 1981, the first in a series of major tax reform acts was enacted, namely: The Economic Recovery Tax Act. The nation was in an economic recession at the time, and tax incentives appeared to be a way to get the country going again. The maximum federal income tax rates were 70%; citizens were desperate for more knowledge in ways to ease the tax bite. It was in this environment that the author decided to develop a whole new series of readably written, selected-subject tax books.

Coming out with anything new takes time, creative effort, prototype samples, and plain old-fashioned trial-and-error. The author formulated his vision of a 25-volume series of "Allyear Tax Guides." The 25 separate subject titles were organized into five miniseries of five titles each. Each book would focus on one taxpayer subject at a time, with in-depth tax information on that one subject. The "in-depth" objective was to cite the applicable tax law, give examples of taxpayer experiences therewith, and relate how the IRS interprets — and misinterprets — the applicable law. Text organization, writing style, diagrams, and tables were to be used to entice readership interest in an otherwise boring and loathsome subject: taxes.

The above objectives necessitated the creation of prototype printed samples of the proposed 25-volume tax book series. The printed samples were necessary to generate reader feedback and critical reviews by prospective publishers. For preparing these samples, the author had to employ the services of commercial artists, book designers, typographers, printers, and book binders.

When the author prepared his 1981 return, he entered the following information on his Schedule C (Form 1040): Profit or Loss from Business or Profession—

R & E Expenses: Sec. 174(a)
- *Prototype 303*   *$16,485*
- *M/S (pasteup) 403*   *6,561*
- *Prototype 403*   *9,048*
- *M/S (pasteup) 203*   *5,640*
- *Prototype 203*   *10,134*
                             $47,868

The IRS auditor(s) went through every invoice for these items, and tallied every cancelled check. The expenditures listed above were verified to the dollar. Nevertheless, an IRS spokesperson for the auditor(s) said (as paraphrased):

"We don't know how to handle research expenses on Schedule C, so we are going to disallow everything. We don't think your expenditures qualify as "technological" research in the laboratory sense. You'll have to take the matter up elsewhere."

> *Editorial Note*: The tax law on point — Section 174(a) — says nothing whatever about the expenditures being "technological" in order to be allowed. The exact wording in the IR Code is: *research or experimental expenditures . . . in connection with* [a taxpayer's] *trade or business.* [Emphasis added.]

Evidently, the IRS felt that writing and preparing sample tax books by a tax return preparer was not "in connection with" his trade or business. Hence, we identify this dispute as: ISSUE II — Prototype Expenses.

Specific Dispute III

When the author above wrote his Issue I letter to the President (May 1981) renouncing his lifetime Social Security benefits, he included a paragraph that read—

Henceforth, no further Social Security taxes will be paid by me, the undersigned, inasmuch as the benefits therefrom, by virtue of this irrevocable renunciation, can never be claimed.

The author's rationale was: "Look, I've contributed my lifetime Social Security benefits to the public good. I've paid into the system for 28 years. Why continue paying when I'm not going to receive any benefits?"

The author, as a tax preparer, was self-employed. This meant that the net earnings on his Schedule C were subject to a second income tax called: Self-Employment Social Security Tax. This requires the preparation of Schedule SE (Form 1040). Accordingly, he prepared his 1981 Schedule SE as follows:

Net earnings (after Issue II expenses)   *$18,319*
Enter adjustments, if any   *<18,319>*
Adjusted net earnings: attach statement   *-0-*

The author circled the preprinted instruction "attach statement" and attached a copy of his Issue I gift letter to the President.

The auditor initially assigned to the case in June, 1984 said nothing about the taxpayer's Schedule SE whatsoever.

Some four months later — on November 5, 1984, to be exact — the managing supervisor of the IRS Special Audits Division phoned the author. He said:

"We're getting sick and tired of you tax preparers around here. You're playing games with the system. There was no gift. Your whole idea is outrageous, preposterous, and frivolous. So much so that we are going to recommend the 50% civil fraud penalty against you."

Obviously, this particular IRS agent, a mid-management level veteran, was irate. The author responded on the telephone:

"There are no elements of fraud here. Fraud requires concealment with intent to evade. If you will look at my 1981 return, there is no concealment of any kind."

Raising his voice and shouting, the IRS agent snapped back:

"That doesn't matter. I'm going to warn you right now: if you claim a charitable deduction for this on your next return, I guarantee I'll turn this over to our Criminal Investigation Division and recommend the 100% criminal fraud penalty in addition to the 50% civil fraud penalty."

End of phone conversation. Hence, we identify this dispute as: ISSUE III — Fraud Penalty.

Specific Dispute IV

Once an IRS agent alleges fraud based on an audit — whether right or wrong — the IRS has instant authority to audit *6 consecutive years* of tax returns (Sec. 6531). This is the big "power play" routine which we depict in Figure 2.2.

As to Issues I, II, and III above, a total of six consecutive years of the author's returns was indeed audited. The years were 1981, 1982, 1983, 1984, 1985, and 1986. The identical issues were in dispute for all years except 1984. That year was a statute-of-limitations fluke.

What happened was that all of the IRS's heavy artillery was brought to bear on 1981. It also went into the author's returns for prior consecutive years as far back as 1972. It couldn't audit the years prior to 1981, but it could use information from any of the earlier years as evidence in its fraud case. The IRS's irate agent and his investigative staff spent so much time on the pre-1981 years that, when they got around to auditing 1984, the statute of limitations had expired for 1984.

Because fraud was asserted, the author engaged a tax attorney and paid the following amounts of attorney fees:

1985	—	$ 1,475
1986	—	3,815
1987	—	20,756
1988	—	10,387
1989	—	27,700
1990	—	23,106
1991	—	5,039

The 7-year total attorney fees came to **$92,278**. These amounts were treated by the author as a business expense and were deducted for the respective years on his Schedule C (Form 1040).

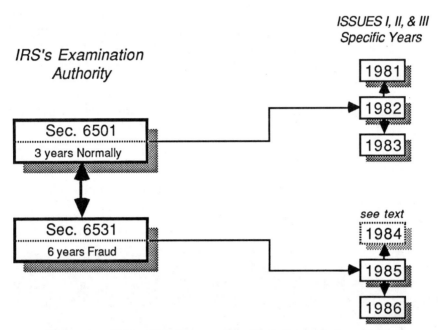

ISSUES I, II, & III
Specific Years

IRS's Examination
Authority

Sec. 6501
3 years Normally

Sec. 6531
6 years Fraud

1981
1982
1983

see text
1984
1985
1986

Fig. 2.2 - IRS's Big "Power Play": 6 Consecutive Years

Issues I, II, and III for years 1981, 1982, and 1983 were Tax Court concluded in 1990. There was imposed on the author a triple-compounding of deficiency interest which totaled **$52,521**. On his 1990 and 1991 returns, the author claimed 60% of the deficiency interest as a business expense attributable to his Schedule C.

Both the 1990 and 1991 returns were IRS audited. Needless to say, the Schedules C attorney fees and deficiency interest were summarily disallowed. We'll designate this dispute as Issue IV — Attorney Fees and Deficiency Interest.

We'll not go any further into Issues I, II, III, and IV in this chapter. We'll do so separately in Chapters 7, 8, 9, and 10. We just want you to get the general picture of how tax disputes come about. Once a bona fide dispute arises, the challenge is to get it heard in Tax Court properly.

3

THE "90-DAY" LETTER(S)

A Two-Page Preprinted NOTICE OF DEFICIENCY By the IRS Is Your Tax Court Cue. You Have 90 Days (NOT 3 Months) To Petition The Court For Redetermination Of The Deficiency And Penalties . . . For Each Tax Year. To Each Notice, The IRS Attaches "Explanations." These Are Stereotyped, One-Paragraph Assertions That YOU Must Prove Wrong. Fraud And Other Penalties Are Frequently Asserted Simply Because There Are NO OBJECTIVE STANDARDS In The IR Code On Penalty Matters. In The Case Of Fraud, The IRS Has The Burden Of Proof . . . BUT ONLY IF You Go All The Way To Trial.

A "90-day" letter is the statutory Notice of Deficiency which the IRS sends you when it can no longer drag out disputed matters. If it wants to levy and seize your bank accounts, etc. (after you have filed your return), it must send you said letter. This must be done **on or prior to:**

A. Expiration of 3 years from the due date of your return, OR
B. Expiration of 90 days after you file Form 872-T terminating your waiver of the 3-year statute, if you had previously signed Form 872-A.

All the IRS has to do is to send the "90-day" letter by certified mail to the latest address that it has for the taxpayer. If the taxpayer's address on the IRS computer is wrong, the IRS is held blameless. All it needs is a receipt for certified mail in its files.

As long as the taxpayer's social security number is correct on the letter, and as long as the IRS can show that it sent it, the IRS can go back to its bureaucratic ways.

Basically, all the 90-day letter says is—

"Yes, there is a dispute between you and the IRS. You have just 90 days — NOT 3 months — to either pay the full amount asserted or file a petition in the U.S. Tax Court."

Of course, there is more to the letter than this, but this is the gist of it. The letter is a formal legal notice that you cannot ignore. If you do, then forget about going into Tax Court.

So, in this chapter, we want to focus on the 90-day (statutory) letter process, its format, its meaning, and its shortcomings. We want to discuss your obligations with respect to it, and follow through with specific example letters that derived from Issues I, II, III, and IV that we introduced to you in Chapter 2.

Meaning of "90 Days"

The meaning of 90 days in an official letter is not quite as self-explanatory as one might think. If it is mailed out by the IRS on March 1st, for example, the 90th day expires on May 30th. March has 31 days, so March 2nd counts as Day 1. April has 30 days, so the count is up to day 60. May has 31 days, so Day 90 occurs on May 30th. It does NOT occur on June 1st, as one might normally think. A 90-day letter is not a 3-month letter.

The letter is an official notification that your rights to petition the U.S. Tax Court expire exactly 90 consecutive days after the date stamped on the letter by the IRS. There are no extensions of the 90 days whatsoever. The situation is unlike filing a tax return where, upon application, you can extend your legal date for filing. Not so for a petition to the Tax Court. If no petition is filed on or before the 90th day, you've lost your case before you start.

If the 90th day ends on a Saturday, Sunday, or national holiday, you had better anticipate the consequences. Technically, the next business day following the weekend or holiday constitutes the 90th day. But be aware that this is a legal fine-point which the IRS will use to invalidate your petition. How do you protect yourself against the legal misdeeds of the IRS?

The answer is that you physically go to the nearest open branch of the U.S. Postal Service, pay the certified mailing fee, and get a receipt. Make absolutely sure that the postal clerk applies a **legible** official USPS stamp to your receipt. We recommend you do this the day preceding the weekend or holiday.

Transmittal of the 90-day letter to you by the IRS is via the U.S. Mail system only. Its deposit in the U.S. Mail starts the legal time ticking. The IRS is not required to send the letter by any other means. If it takes five days for delivery, or 25 days, your legal days for counting start with the date officially stamped on the letter by the IRS. The IRS dating is construed to be coincident with its depositing the letter in the U.S. Mail. We know that this is not always the case, but taxpayers have no way of disproving the IRS. This dating issue has been court tested. As frequently happens, federal courts are more protective of the powers of the IRS than of the rights of individual taxpayers.

If you use the U.S. Mail for delivering your Tax Court petition, all you have to do is get it into the mail system on or before the 90th day. Don't forget a legible certified mail receipt. If the U.S. Mail takes 30 days, or whatever, for delivery, you are legally covered. It is your *deposit* in the U.S. Mail that counts: NOT its delivery.

On the other hand, if you do not use the U.S. Mail system, your petition must be *delivered* to the U.S. Tax Court on or before the 90th day. You cannot use a postage meter, private mailing, fax, or other express service, and treat the date of contract as date of deposit in the U.S. Mail.

The Statutory Requirements

The 90-day letter is a document of profound legal importance in the enforcement and collection of tax by the IRS. After 90 days, and there is no petition to the Tax Court, awesome powers of the IRS are unleashed. For one, the IRS is not held to any truth in tax, or to correct tax standards. It can — AND DOES — magnify the alleged deficiency severalfold; it can — AND DOES — pyramid all applicable penalties. For a document with such profound power behind it, it is disturbing to see how minimal the statutory requirements are on the IRS.

Officially, a 90-day letter is called: **Notice of Deficiency**. This is the designation assigned to it by Section 6212 of the IR Code. The essence of this statutory notice is found in subsection 6212(a). This subsection reads in essential part as—

If the [IRS] determines that there is a deficiency in respect of any tax . . . [the IRS] is authorized to send notice of such deficiency to the taxpayer by certified mail.

Let us analyze this tax code section for a moment. Look how weak it is in protecting the taxpayer against IRS abuses. There are no standards for determining a deficiency. Does the IRS have to determine the correct deficiency or correct penalty . . . or just any deficiency or any penalty? The judicial answer is: "ANY deficiency, ANY penalty," whether correct or not. There is no prohibition whatsoever against the IRS for magnifying and manufacturing deficiencies and penalties. Surely, since 1954 when Section 6212 was first enacted, somebody in Congress or on the President's staff must have wondered about protecting the taxpayer in some manner. Evidently not.

The result is that the IRS has no obligation to make reasonably correct "determinations" in its Notice of Deficiency. The only obligation it has is to send the deficiency notice to the taxpayer's "last known address" [Sec. 6212(b)(1)]. If the taxpayer filed a joint return, and the spouses live at *separate residences*, the IRS is authorized to send duplicates of the joint notice to each of the separate addresses. So long as a certified mail notice is not returned to the IRS by the U.S. Mail system as being undeliverable, the presumption is that the notice was indeed received by the taxpayer.

Subsection 6212(c)(1) provides another opening for abuse by the IRS, which neither the Congress nor the President has sought to address. The specific statutory phrase for concern is—

*If the [IRS] has mailed . . . a notice of deficiency . . . and the taxpayer files a petition with the Tax Court within the time prescribed . . . the [IRS] shall have no right to determine any additional deficiency . . . **except in the case of fraud.** [Emphasis added.]*

There is great danger in this fraud exception for additional deficiencies. There are NO OBJECTIVE STANDARDS whatever in the tax code as to what constitutes fraud. There are no IRS regulations either, setting forth a checklist of the "indices of fraud." The determination of fraud by the IRS rests *solely and exclusively* on the personal whim and vindictiveness of the IRS agent initiating the allegation.

The above "no objective standards" statement is not recklessly made. Clear evidence of the whim and vindictiveness of the IRS agent will become apparent from trial testimony (cited in Chapter 9).

Effect of Filing Petition

There is reason why a Notice of Deficiency is not officially called a "90-day letter." There is also statutory provision for 150 days for addresses located outside the U.S. On the matter of foreign addresses, Section 6213(a): Time for Filing Petition, says—

Within 90 days, or 150 days if the notice is addressed to a person outside the United States, after the notice of deficiency . . . is mailed.

This tax code section is a remarkable revelation in itself. The powers of the IRS regarding its allegations of deficiency or fraud extend throughout the entire world!

If the addressee of a deficiency notice responds timely and files a petition with the U.S. Tax Court, what protection against the IRS does a petition-filer have?

Answer: Section 6213(a) says in further part—

No assessment of a deficiency in respect of any tax . . . and no levy or proceeding in court for its collection shall be made, begun, or prosecuted . . . until the decision of the Tax Court has become final.

Thus, the only protection you get with a Tax Court petition is a stay (suspension) of collection enforcement by the IRS. Unfortunately, this protection does not extend to the suspension of the daily compounding of interest while under the Tax Court's jurisdiction. Here, again, the Congress and the President have produced a legislative oversight. The IRS takes advantage of this oversight by dragging out the TC proceeding as long as it can.

What does the IRS gain by dragging its feet in Tax Court?

Obviously, you are not aware of Section 6214(a): Jurisdiction as to Increase of Deficiency, Additional Amounts, or Additions to the Tax. The essence of this gem is—

*The Tax Court shall have jurisdiction to . . . determine whether any additional amount, or **any addition to the tax** should be* *assessed, if claim therefor is **asserted** by the* [IRS] *at or before the hearing or rehearing.* [Emphasis added.]

The emphasized phrase "any addition to the tax" means: ANY penalty, in ANY amount, in ANY repetitiveness. By dragging a case out, the IRS can — and does — harp at the court to consider additional allegations and assertions that are *not* in the initial Notice of Deficiency. Being a "brother agency" to the Tax Court, the IRS is allowed more prerogatives in this regard than any counter allegations by the taxpayer.

Notice Form & Contents

A 90-day letter — otherwise known as Notice of Deficiency — is a two-page, preprinted document officially designated as Letter 531. It pretends to explain your rights for petitioning the Tax Court if you do not agree with the amount of tax deficiency and penalties asserted. It offers the opportunity of not petitioning the Tax Court, by signing the enclosed statute-of-limitation waiver forms. The only protection signing a waiver gives you is that the IRS will send its demand for payment (plus compounded interest) by regular mail, rather than levying your bank and taking it. If you petition the Tax Court, you can disregard the waiver form.

Instead of reciting the entire letter verbatim, we present you with a generalized format of the notice letter, and point to the key items that you should read. We do this in Figure 3.1. For quick-identity purposes, we have numbered the paragraph blocks in Figure 3.1, whereas they are unnumbered on the official notice.

Over the years, the IRS has made a conscientious effort to soften the threatening language of its official notices. But it still can't resist booming penalties at you. It is an ingrown addiction to power which the tax system cannot shake. When penalties are imposed, they appear at the head of the letter, where you see the penalties before you see the letter text.

The upper right-hand corner of the letter states the legal essentials: your social security number, the tax year for which a deficiency is asserted, the amount of the deficiency, and the amount and code section of the asserted penalties. If your social security number is correct, and you received the letter within 90 days of its certified mail date, the IRS has you cornered.

The only way out of the corner is to read — and reread — the second paragraph of the letter. It gives you incomplete instructions

Internal Revenue Service Department of the Treasury	Social Security Number _____
Date _____	Tax Year_____ Deficiency_____ Penalty 1 $_____
Certified Mail	Penalty 2 $_____ Penalty 3 $_____
Adressee _____ _____ _____	Person to Contact _____ _____

Dear Taxpayer:

1.	NOTICE OF DEFICIENCY & enclosed statement
2.	90 DAYS (or 150 DAYS if outside U.S.) _____ To Contest, MUST PETITION U.S. Tax Court_____ Instructions for signing petition_____
3.	Instructions: Small tax cases_____
4.	Instructions: If no contest, sign waiver_____
5.	If questions, phone or write_____

Enclosures

● **Statement**

● **Waiver**

Commissioner, IRS

by _____ /s/ _____

_____ name _____

_____ title _____

Fig. 3.1 - General Format of Notice of Deficiency

about filing a petition in the Tax Court. It gives the address, but not the phone number. It does not tell you that you have to prepare a special petition form and that you need to contact the Clerk of the Court for the form and for the court's rules of procedure. Nor does it tell you that you have to pay a $60 filing fee to the Tax Court. In addition to attaching a waiver form for you to sign, the IRS — if it were truly serving the public — should attach a summary sheet explaining the petition form, fee, and phone numbers in Washington, D.C., together with a Tax Court petition form for you to use, if you so desire.

Duplicate Letters for Fraud

When the IRS alleges fraud — right or wrong — it can send duplicate deficiency letters to each of the spouses filing a joint return. There is a special rule on this point, namely: Section 6663(c): Fraud Penalty for Joint Returns. This rule reads as—

In the case of a joint return, this section [6663: Imposition of Fraud Penalty] *shall not apply with respect to a spouse **unless some part** of the underpayment is due to the fraud of such spouse.* [Emphasis added.]

As to Issue III presented previously, the 1981 return was filed jointly (as were all subsequent returns). The husband was the "culprit" who wrote, signed, and notarized the 1981 letter to the President renouncing, irrevocably, his lifetime Social Security benefits as a public gift. It was quite clear from the shouting phone threats by the IRS spokesperson (Group Manager) in November, 1984 that the civil fraud and criminal investigation penalties would be asserted against the husband. Nothing was said about any fraud being committed by the wife.

Willing to cooperate with the IRS in its fraud investigation, the spouses signed the Special Consent Form 872-A extending the statute of limitations for their 1981 return. The statute was due to expire April 15, 1985. The matter then went to IRS Appeals.

1988 came and the taxpayers were growing tired of the IRS's foot dragging. They prepared and signed form 872-T for terminating the above open-ended waiver. This was done in February, 1988.

Two days later, the wife received a 1981 deficiency letter in her name and social security number only. The notice displayed the following:

Deficiency for 1981 $24,050
Fraud Penalty $14,525

Just below this information was the name of the IRS appeals officer and phone number to contact.

The taxpayer (husband) phoned the appeals officer and asked why his wife was being penalized for fraud. The IRS response was (as paraphrased):

"By your own admission, your wife typed your letter to the President. That makes her a conspirator to fraud."

"Oh, come on. Be reasonable. If I had a public stenographer type the letter, would that be a conspiracy to fraud?"

IRS's answer: "That's a different story. Your wife signed the joint return with you, so she's liable for fraud. That's the way it's gonna be!"

The 6-Year Barrage

Two months after the wife's deficiency notice was mailed, a barrage of other 90-day letters came out of the IRS's woodwork. The first such was a separate 1981 deficiency notice addressed to the husband only (in his social security number). Here's side-by-side comparison of the two spousal notices (ACTUAL FIGURES):

	Wife (2/88)	Husband (4/88)
1981 Deficiency	$24,050	$24,814
Fraud Penalty	$14,525	$12,407

Do you see anything curious here?

The wife's fraud penalty is some $2,000 greater than the husband's fraud penalty. She's an ordinary housewife with no separate income of her own.

The husband was the one who renounced his Social Security benefits (the wife didn't do this). The husband claimed the charitable deduction for his lifetime gift, and discontinued paying his self-employment social security tax. So, how come the wife is fraud penalized $2,000 more?

Be whatever may. Four other deficiency notices were received by the taxpayers relating to Issues I, II, and III for years 1982 through 1986. These additional notices were in joint names; they were not duplicates for each, as above.

A digest of all six deficiency notices is presented in Figure 3.2. These are the actual official deficiency and penalty amounts; they are NOT hypothetical examples. For impact purposes, we have totaled

Tax Year	Statutory Date	Waiver Date	Notice Date	Deficiency Asserted	Fraud Penalty	Other Penalties
1981 (W)	4/85	2/88	2/88	$24,050	$14,525	$
1981 (H)	4/85	2/88	4/88	24,817	12,407	
1982	4/86	2/88	4/88	20,893	10,447	8,381
1983	4/87	2/88	4/88	20,729	10,365	8,889
1984	4/88					
1985	4/89		9/88	8,633		2,590
1986	4/90		10/88	19,283		5,785
		Totals		118,405	47,744	25,645
		GRAND TOTAL ▶			$191,794	

Fig. 3.2 - Noticed Deficiencies & Penalties: Issues I, II, & III

the amounts in all six notices. You may want to come back to Figure 3.2 much later, after you are apprised of the Tax Court decisions.

There is one particular noteworthy item in Figure 3.2. It is the absence of the fraud penalty for tax years 1985 and 1986. There's a special story behind this which will come out in the description of the trial. But, we'll tip you off now. The IRS amended its 1985 and 1986 notices, and *added* the fraud penalties just before trial began. The added fraud penalties were $4,317 for 1985 and $14,462 for 1986.

In all six of the Figure 3.2 deficiency notices, the same issues threaded through. For refresher purposes, these issues were:

ISSUE I   — Public Gift: Schedule A
ISSUE II   — Prototype Expenses: Schedule C
ISSUE III — Fraud Penalty: Schedule SE

Attached to each of the six notices, the IRS provided "explanations" for its determinations.

IRS Explanation: Issue I

Issue I is the matter of the husband (at age 62) gifting his lifetime social security benefits to the public at large. He did this via a renunciatory letter addressed to the President dated May 12, 1981. This was followed by his Congressman forwarding the letter on June 23, 1981 to the Social Security Administration for recording.

On the 1981 joint return, the husband computed his actuarial social security benefits for his remaining life to be $88,583. He annotated the charitable contributions portion of his Schedule A (Itemized Deductions) with specific reference to IR Code **Section 170(c)(1)**.

For background purposes, Section 170(c)(1) reads as—

Sec. 170. Charitable, Etc., Contributions and Gifts
(c) Charitable Contribution Defined—
For purposes of this section, the term "charitable contribution" means a contribution or gift to or for the use of—
(1) A state, a possession of the United States, or any political subdivision of any of the foregoing, or the United States or the District of Columbia, but only if the contribution or gift is made for exclusively public purposes.

This is the applicable tax law which Congress passed and the President signed. This is the law that the IRS is supposed to uphold and respect. It is supposed to apply reasonable standards of interpretation, and not create new interpretations of its own. Sure, there are some nuances involved. For example, what does a *contribution or gift* mean?

Now for the IRS's official explanation supporting its deficiency notice. The IRS's exact words read in full as—

It has been determined that the $88,583 shown on your 1981 return as a deduction for charitable contributions is not allowable in full because it has not been established that the total amount was paid during the tax year or that the unallowable items met the requirements of section 170 of the Internal Revenue Code. Accordingly, your taxable income is increased.

Except for modifications in the years and the respective-year carryover amounts, the same explanation applied to 1982, 1983, 1985, and 1986.

It should be pointed out that the taxpayers' joint 1981 return was filed in January 1982. The notice of deficiency to the wife was dated February 1988. This is a full six years after the original return was filed!

Stripped of its bureaucratic veneer, what the IRS is really saying (and getting away with) is—

"We disallowed it because we are the IRS, and the burden of proof is on *you*, taxpayer, to prove us wrong."

IRS Explanation: Issue II

Issue II is the matter of the husband, a tax return preparer (the author herein), inaugurating an all-new 25-volume series of readable tax books. The editorial objectives were to state the applicable tax laws on selected subjects, then discuss the IRS's practices, tax forms, and interpretations/misinterpretations therewith. He was targeting a new readership between the once-a-year populist tax guides and the once-a-week professional tax updates. He was striving for the "middle ground" with his own writing creativity and diagrammatic presentations. He paid for the preparation of printed samples (prototypes) of his intended tax books. He used the samples for soliciting reader feedback and publisher critiques. It was a trial-and-error experimental ordeal.

On his 1981 return (and subsequent year returns), the husband isolated on Schedule C (Profit or Loss from Business) all of his prototype expenditures. The separately identified expenditures for 1981 were $47,868. He expressly annotated the applicable lines with reference to IR Code **Section 174(a)(1)**.

This specifically referenced code section reads in full as—

Sec. 174. Research and Experimental Expenditures
 (a) Treatment as Expenses—
  (1) A taxpayer may treat research or experimental expenditures which are paid or incurred by him during the taxable year in connection with his trade or business as expenses which are not chargeable to capital account. The expenses so treated shall be allowed as a deduction.

Again, this is tax law that Congress and the President enacted. The IRS has no authority to alter the intent of such law, by taking a contrary position to that of Congress and the President. But this is PR theory. In practice, the IRS has extraconstitutional authority to ignore any law that it wants, under the guise of maximum revenue. We have in Issue II a perfect example of the IRS's authority to ignore Congress and the President.

The IRS's official explanation supporting its deficiency notice reads in full as—

It has been determined that the $47,868 shown on your return for 1981 as a deduction for Prototype Expenses is not allowable in full because expenses incurred in establishing a business before the time business begins must be capitalized rather than deducted in the year incurred. Accordingly, your taxable income is increased.

Except for modifications in the years and respective-year expenditure amounts, the same explanation applied to 1982, 1983, 1985, and 1986.

Congress's law says: ***not chargeable to capital account.*** The IRS's law says: *must be capitalized.* This is contradictory.

IRS Explanation: Issue III

Issue III is the fraud penalty. It was imposed four times against the noticed taxpayers, as revealed in Figure 3.2. Later, the ante was raised to *six* fraud penalties (totaling $66,523). The objective reasons for doing so are not fully clear. Apparently, the genesis of the issue is the husband's contributing his lifetime Social Security benefits to the general public. He then unilaterally ceased further self-employment Social Security tax contributions. He had already paid the Social Security tax for the previous 28 years. Somewhere in this scenario, the act of fraud was committed. So the IRS alleged.

For instructional background, we find it necessary to cite those portions of the tax code which specifically address fraud by individuals. There are two such IR Code sections, namely:

Sec. 6663(a) — If any part of any underpayment of tax required to be shown on a return is due to fraud, there shall be added to the tax an amount equal to [50% prior to 1987] 75 percent of the portion of the underpayment attributable to fraud.

Sec. 7454(a) — In any proceeding involving the issue whether the petitioner has been guilty of fraud with intent to evade tax, the burden of proof in respect of such issue shall be upon the [IRS].

> **Editorial Note**: Where we have inserted the letters "IRS" in brackets above, the actual code wording says "Secretary." This is the Secretary of Treasury of which the IRS is part. This was displayed to you back in Figure 1.1.

So much for statutory background. What is the IRS's explanation of the fraud that it found on the tax returns identified above?

These are the IRS's EXACT WORDS:

Since all or part of the underpayment of tax required to be shown on your return is due to fraud, a penalty of 50 percent of the underpayment is added to the tax. [33 words.]

This same 33-word explanation accompanied the deficiency notices for 1981(H), 1981(W), 1982(J), 1983(J), 1985(J), and 1986(J). [H = husband; W = wife; J = joint.]

THAT's an explanation of the fraud committed by the taxpayers! That's an explanation for wanting $66,523 in fraud penalties!

IRS Explanation: Issue IV

The Tax Court decisions on Issues I, II, and III were rendered on June 30, 1990 for years 1981, 1982, and 1983; and on December 12, 1990 for years 1985 and 1986. By the time all of the post-trial papers were in, and the amount of tax "redetermined," all of 1990 and 1991 had gone by. That's a span of 11 years! Over this span of time, the total attorney fees paid amounted to $92,278 and the amount of deficiency interest assessed by the IRS was $52,521 . . . plus $4,781 assessed by California (total: $57,302).

In an attempt to recoup some of these expenses, the author entered on his 1990 and 1991 Schedules C: Profit or Loss from Business, the following amounts:

	Attorney Fees	Deficiency Interest
1990	$23,106	$31,628
1991	5,039	2,879
	$28,145	$34,507

The attorney fees are $64,133 less than the $92,278 cited previously (92,278 − 28,145 = 64,133). This is because $64,133 was included on Schedules C over the years 1985 through 1989 as they were being paid.

The deficiency interest was all paid in years 1990 and 1991. The amount entered on the Schedules C constitutes 60.22% of the actual amounts paid. The 60.22% is the portion "allocable" to Schedule C, whereas the remainder 39.78% was allocable to Schedule A. Schedule A represents personal deductions, whereas Schedule C represents business deductions.

In 1992, the IRS audited the 1990 and 1991 returns, and summarily disallowed the Schedule C entries above. This is where the saga of Issue IV — Attorney Fees, Etc., begins.

After indicating his disagreement with the auditor, the author requested that a 90-day letter: Notice of Deficiency, be issued immediately. About a year later, February 18, 1993, he received said letter.

The deficiencies were noted as—

1990   — $7,737
1991   — $3,386 + $94 penalty

Keep this $94 penalty in mind. It will come up in Chapter 10 (At Trial: Issue IV) for "penalty smearing" purposes. The notice letter was accompanied by 15 pages of computations and two "explanation" sentences.

The IRS's explanation for disallowing the $28,145 in attorney fees was—

The expense is not an allowable deduction at this time due to the fact that the origins of the expense need to be determined and the allocation then to be made. Also, a portion of the expense is a double deduction and not attributable to a trade or business: it is personal.

For reference purposes, Section 162(a) of the IR Code says—

*There shall be allowed as a deduction all the ordinary and necessary expenses paid or incurred during the taxable years **in carrying on any** trade or business.* [Emphasis added.]

The IRS's explanation for disallowing the $34,507 in deficiency interest was—

Since the interest was on a contested liability and the interest was for prior years . . . this expense is related to your personal income tax and belongs on Schedule A. The deduction has been allowed on Schedule A 1990 at 10% [and 1991 at 0%].

Editorial Note: The Tax Reform Act of 1986 "phased-out" (over a 4-year period) all personal interest deductions on Schedule A except for qualified mortgage interest.

Again, for reference purposes, Section 163(h): Disallowance of Deduction for Personal Interest, says—

The term "personal interest" means any interest allowable as a deduction . . . other than—
    *(A) interest paid or accrued on indebtedness **properly allocable** to a trade or business.* [Emphasis added.]

All Total: Three Trials

Issues I, II, and III were heard, redundantly, in two separate trials; Issue IV was heard in a trial of its own. Thus, altogether, there were three separate Tax Court trials, namely:

Trial I   — heard: March 14, 1989
Trial II   — heard: December 5, 1989
Trial III   — heard: February 18, 1994

Trial I addressed years 1981, 1982, and 1983; Trial II addressed years 1985 and 1986; Trial III addressed years 1990 and 1991. The final decision on Trial III was not rendered until August 1995. In other words, the whole first-hand "testing episode" by the author spanned a total of 15 years: 1981 through 1995.

For each Tax Court trial, there has to be at least one 90-day letter. For Trial I, there were *four* such letters; for Trial II, there were two; for Trial III, there was one. This totaled seven 90-day letters. Although the author was able to sort these out intelligently, the IRS and the Tax Court were confused in what they were focusing on. This is because the underlying adversarial tactic used by the IRS is to confuse the disputed issues as much as possible.

4

PETITION, ANSWER, & REPLY

A PETITION To The Tax Court Starts The "Pleading Phase" Of Your Dispute. The General Format And Contents Are Prescribed By The Court, The Meat Of Which Is In Paragraphs 4 (Assignment Of Errors) And 5 (Statement Of Facts). Within 60 To 120 Days, The IRS Must ANSWER Your Petition, Point By Point. It Routinely Denies Everything And Asserts That The Tax Laws On Which You Rely Are Irrelevant. Then The IRS Adds A FURTHER Answer By Raising New Allegations And Assertions. You Must REPLY To These Point By Point, Otherwise The New Allegations Are "Deemed Admitted." Eventually, The Disputive Issues Are "Joined."

Upon receiving a Notice of Deficiency, there is one clear and immediate task to do. Phone or write to the Clerk of the Tax Court (address on the Notice), and request a copy of the TC Rules of Procedure and sample petition forms. Don't delay on this. There are no extensions of time for filing a TC Petition.

Meanwhile, start formulating your thoughts for your petition contents. Although some procedural formality is required, the main thrust of a Petition has to do with what is called: **assignment of errors**. One cannot assert that the IRS was arbitrary and ill motivated. In many cases, the IRS is truly arbitrary; it has the power to say "No," without giving satisfactory explanation. For some reason, TC judges take offense when you accuse the IRS of being arbitrary and mean-spirited. The presumption is that the IRS may have made errors in its deficiency notices, but these were never done arbitrarily. Therefore, you have to "assign errors" to the deficiency issues asserted by the IRS.

Between the date of the Notice and the date the Petition is set for hearing, a lot of "papers" go back and forth. There are papers from you to the Tax Court, from the Tax Court to the IRS, from you to the IRS, from the IRS to you, and from the IRS to the Tax Court. This is all part of the pre-calendaring process called the *pleading phase* of your dispute. All of this pleading business takes place in the domain of the Clerk of the Court. Eventually, the issues are joined and a trial date is set.

In this chapter, we want to focus on the contents of a petition and on the joinder aspects of Issues I, II, and III. (We'll defer the petition contents on Issue IV to Chapter 10. Issue IV is post-climactic.) Technically, the purpose of the pleading and joinder phase of TC proceedings is to narrow down the issues, refine them, and set objective standards by which they can be judged. This is more theory than practice. The TC Rules do not recognize the unlevel playing field when the IRS is involved. When we get to the IRS's answer to a petition, you'll see what we mean.

Procedural Overview

Once you have received a Notice of Deficiency from the IRS, and you wish to seek a redetermination of the tax at issue, you "switch the track" and proceed under the Tax Court rules. You are no longer under the dominance and control of the IRS. You engage in a series of what are called *pleadings*. The purpose of the pleadings is to give fair notice to the Court and to the IRS of the matters in controversy and the basis for your position.

There is a 4-step pleading process that must be completed before the issues in dispute are "joined." The first such step is the IRS notice itself. This notice is a pleading to the Court that: "We [the IRS] have determined that . . . ." The second pleading is your petition requesting redetermination of the amount alleged by the IRS. The third pleading is an answer to your petition by the IRS that your position on the issue(s) is misinformed. The fourth pleading is your reply to the IRS's answer that the IRS has misinterpreted the law as it exists in the tax code.

A diagram of this 4-step pleading process is presented in Figure 4.1. As indicated, the particularly applicable Tax Court rules are identified. We have indicated also the time allowed between the

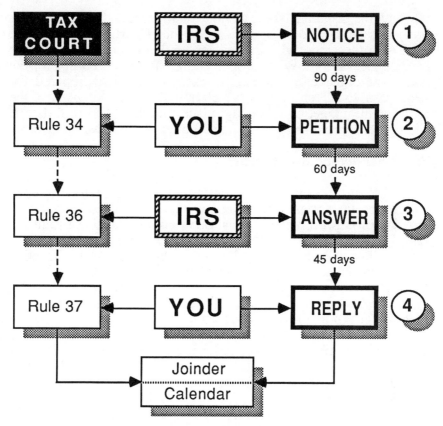

Fig. 4.1 - The Pleading Process for "Joinder" of Issues

pleadings. Except for the 90 days for petition filing (150 days when out of the country), the other times may be extended upon request to the Court. It is the IRS that requests most of the extensions.

The pleading papers have to meet a certain form and style; they must be signed and dated; and they must carry the document number assigned to the petition by the Clerk of the Court. The document number is not assigned until the petition is received in Washington, D.C., together with—

1. A filing fee (currently $60)
2. A copy of the Notice of Deficiency
3. Current address of the pleader
4. Legible signature of the petitioner or his counsel

Until the disputive issues are joined, all pleading pages and their acceptances are handled by the Clerk of the Court. The papers are filed with the clerk, who in turn serves them upon the opposing party as necessary. When the pleading papers are complete, the issues are considered joined. A case file is then prepared for assignment to a Trial Judge. The clerk will notify each party of the name of the judge, and date and place for trial. The trial date is initially set approximately nine months after the issues are joined.

Petition Format & Contents

Ordinarily, a separate petition is required for each deficiency notice, for each year. However, when the issues are similar or repetitive for two or more years, one petition can serve multiple years (and multiple notices). Whether one petition or two (or three), each shall be complete in its own right. This is so that all disputive matters on the same issue or set of issues are in one place. No telegram, cablegram, radiogram, telephone call, electronically transmitted copy, or similar communication will be recognized as a "petition," even though headed as such.

Rule 34(b) sets forth in detail the required contents of a recognized petition. This rule urges use of the format provided in the appendix to the TC Rules of Procedure. We introduce this format in Figure 4.2. The basic contents required are shown in abbreviated form.

The standard leadoff paragraph to every petition reads as follows:

The petitioner hereby petitions for a redetermination of the deficiency set forth by the Commissioner of Internal Revenue in the Commissioner's notice of deficiency [reference symbols, if any] *dated_____, and as the basis for the petitioner's case alleges as follows:*

1. _____)	
2. _____)	
3. _____)	[Separately numbered paragraphs]
4. _____)	
5. _____)	

Paragraph 1 identifies the petitioner by his social security number and address, and identifies the IRS office where the petitioner filed his tax return for the year(s) at issue. Paragraph 2

```
.................................                    .................................
:    Petitioner      :                    :    Space for       :
:   OR Attorney      :                    :  Official Stamp    :
:  Address & Phone   :                    :   of the Court     :
.................................                    .................................
```

UNITED STATES TAX COURT

```
....................................................................        )
          Petitioner(s)                      )
               v.                            )   DOCKET NO. _____
Commissioner of Internal Revenue,            )
          Respondent                         )
_____ )
```

PETITION

The Petitioner(s) hereby ....

1. Identification and social security numbers ....

2. Copy of Notice of Deficiency and date ....

3. Amount of deficiency, year, and amount in dispute...................................

4. **Assignment of Errors**..
           A. Issue I   C. Issue III
           B. Issue II D. Issue X

5. **Statement of Facts**..
           A. Issue I   C. Issue III
           B. Issue II D. Issue X

WHEREFORE, petitioner(s) pray that ....

Dated: _____   _____/s/_____

                                    Petitioner(s)
                                    OR Attorney
                                    TC No. _____

Fig. 4.2 - General Format & Contents of Petition

identifies the IRS office which issued the deficiency notice, and attaches a copy of said notice as Exhibit A. Paragraph 3 recites the amount of deficiency and penalty for each year, and whether all or part of each year is in dispute. Paragraphs 4 and 5 are discussed separately below.

All petitions end with a prayer for relief. A "prayer" is a statement of the decision which the petitioner is urging upon the court. One prays for determination of no deficiency, reduced deficiency, no penalty, or overpayment of tax. The relief sought must be expressly identified as a way of signing off on the petition.

A petition may be amended only once, and then only *before* the IRS responds with its answer (as depicted in Figure 4.1). Amended petitions should be for good and just cause, such as new material facts coming to light.

Rules for Paragraphs 4 and 5

The real meat of a petition is concentrated in Paragraphs 4 and 5. Paragraph 4 addresses the "assignment of errors," whereas Paragraph 5 provides the "statement of facts" in support of those errors. The TC rules on point are Rules 34(b)(4) and (5), respectively.

Rule 34(b)(4) holds that a petitioner must allege **each and every error** that the IRS made when it "determined" a deficiency. There are no limits to the number of errors that can be alleged, so long as each is in good faith and relevant to the tax or penalty in dispute. Each assignment of error should be separately lettered: (a), (b), (c), etc.

Each error should consist of a concise, simple conclusion on each element of a particular issue. All elements of all issues which the petitioner intends to litigate should be raised. This includes issues not raised in the notice of deficiency and those rare issues upon which the IRS has the burden of proof (such as fraud). The petition is your **one and only** chance to get your bona fide complaints on the Tax Court table.

If an error by the IRS is not raised in the petition, the item to which it would have been assigned will be lost. The TC rule on this point is very clear, to wit:

Any issue not raised in the assignment of errors shall be deemed to be conceded.

In other words, the court will not hear that portion of an issue, even if there is good cause for bringing it up later.

As petitioner, you may raise **any factor** which affects the computation of tax (or penalty) in the year(s) covered by the deficiency notice(s). At this point in the pleadings, the matters in controversy are not officially before the court. Therefore, all matters favorable to the petitioner should be included in Paragraph 4.

Rule 34(b)(5) addresses Paragraph 5. This rule requires that there be—

Clear and concise lettered statements of the facts on which petitioner bases the assignments of error.

Insofar as practicable, the statement of facts should be subdivided into a single operative fact or set of facts. Characterization of facts by adverbs and adjectives should be avoided. For example, characterizing the IRS as "willfully arrogant," "carelessly arbitrary," or "without good-faith standards" is offensive to the court. Invariably, it will rise to defend the IRS. The idea is that each set of uncharacterized facts should correlate with the same designating letter used for assignment of errors in Paragraph 4.

Detailed pleading in Paragraph 5 is favored. Such detailing will more sharply define the particular points of disagreement. Although detailed pleading gives the IRS more information on the petitioner's theory and plan of proof, it will require that the IRS be more specific in its denials and spurious claims of "lacking sufficient information" to admit or deny.

Failure to allege the necessary facts supporting each assignment of error may lead the court to enter an order striking out that assignment of error. Once an assignment of error is stricken, the petitioner loses on that point. Without facts supporting each error, there is "no cause of action" for judicial decision. One of the common ploys of the IRS is to request the court to dismiss as many of your pleadings as possible, on the grounds of your "failure to state a cause of action." If you don't provide the tie-in facts to the IRS errors that you have alleged, your cause of action is incomplete. Hence, Paragraphs 4 and 5 must dovetail into each other like fingers in a glove.

Multiple Issues: Same Petition

In complex disputes, multiple issues require careful organization of petition Paragraphs 4 and 5. Probably the best way to do this is to arrange each paragraph into capital-alphabetized parts and parenthesized numerical subparts so that there is a symbolic correlation between Paragraph 4 (errors) and Paragraph 5 (facts). The arrangement could be such as:

A. ___Issue I___
   (1)_____
   (2)_____, etc.
B. ___Issue II___
   (1)_____
   (2)_____, etc.
C. ___Issue III___
   (1)_____
   (2)_____, etc.

Our intent is to illustrate this organization arrangement of a petition for specific issues I, II, and III that we previously identified. As we do so, we will emphasize Paragraphs 4 and 5, and the IRS's point-by-point "answers" thereto.

When the IRS answers a petition, it can add additional paragraphs such as 6, 7, 8, and so on. It does this when it wants to up the ante on existing penalties or add new penalties for fallback purposes.

Petition Example I

The following excerpts are taken directly from an actual petition filed by the author in the U.S. Tax Court on April 28, 1988, docketed as Case No. 8579-88.

Paragraph 4: The determination of tax set forth in the said notice of deficiency is based upon the following errors in law:

A. As to Issue I (Public Gift)—

(1) It is an error to disregard the legislative intent of Public Law 92-603, at Section 132(g), which authorizes any monetary gift or bequest to the Social Security Administration, when voluntarily made.

(2) It is an error to disregard the judicial precedent of Nelson A. Story, III (1962) 38 TC 936 which holds that the cancellation or forgiving of a legal debt obligation constitutes valid "payment" under IRC Sec. 170, fully deductible in the year of cancellation. [IRC is Internal Revenue Code.]

*(3) It is an error to disregard respondent's own Revenue Ruling 82-169, promulgated **after** the petitioner's 1981 gift, which allows such contribution in full, for purposes of IRC Sec. 170(c)(1).*

(4) It is an error to disregard the Social Security Administration's valuation of petitioner's gift of $85,100 and to concurrently disregard its proportionate allocation to years 1981, 1982, and 1983 pursuant to IRC Secs. 170(b) and (d).

Paragraph 5*: The facts upon which the petitioner relies, as the basis of his case, are as follows:*
*A. **As to Issue I (Public Gift)***

(1) For 28 years (112 quarters) prior to 1981, petitioner (H) paid money to the Social Security Administration. All of this money was accepted and credited to his cumulative earnings account.

*(2) In January 1981, petitioner (H) became age 62. As a consequence, pursuant to 42 USC 414(a), he became "fully insured" and legally entitled to monthly payments of money **from** the U.S. Treasury for the rest of his life.*

(3) In 1981, the Social Security System was facing a fiscal crisis. The chairman of the Senate Social Security Subcommittee publicized that—

"Social Security is going broke. Unless decisive action is taken, the trust funds will soon be unable to make ends meet; the Social Security System will be destroyed."

*(4) In 1981, petitioner (H) contacted his Congressman's office and discussed his desire to make a public gift of his entire lifetime entitlement to Social Security benefits. He was told that a "new law" (1972) would permit this. This new law [Sec. 132(g) of P.L. 92-603] recognizes unconditional money gifts to the Social Security Administration as **made for exclusively public purposes**. This latter phrase is exactly the same as that used in IRC Sec. 170(c)(1).*

(5) Other than the "exclusively public purposes" phrase, petitioner (H) could find no IRS regulation, ruling, or procedure which implemented the legislative intent of Sec. 132(g) of P.L. 92-603. To this date, the respondent has published no guidelines — none whatsoever — as to how the petitioner should otherwise have made his intended public gift.

(6) Instead of applying for his monthly entitlements to money from the U.S. Treasury, petitioner (H) on May 12, 1981 renounced irrevocably his lifetime benefits as a public gift "to those in greater need." He did this in a notarized letter addressed to the President of the United States: a legal representative of the Social Security Administration.

Ideally, and on legal theory, each assignment of error in Paragraph 4 should be paralleled with one statement of fact in Paragraph 5. But, as you can see from the above, such idealization is not readily attainable. Errors and facts do not always correlate one-on-one. In the practical world, so long as the correlation is on the designated issue, the listing of errors and facts need only follow some logical sequence.

Petition Example II

Contrast the above with the following example: Issue II. In Issue II, we have ample legislative intent, judicial rulings, and IRS regulations to support the position taken by the taxpayer. Nevertheless, the IRS chose to ignore all of this — quite arbitrarily, we believe — just to give the petitioner (a tax preparer) "a hard time."

At any rate, from Tax Court Docket No. 8579-88, the following excerpts are taken:

Paragraph 4:—
 B . As to Issue II (Prototype Expenses)
  (1) It is an error to disregard the legislative intent of IRC Sec. 174(a) which expressly authorizes the petitioner to elect — without consent — to expense his experimental expenditures "paid or incurred" **in connection with his trade or business.**

  (2) It is an error to disregard the Supreme Court's ruling in Snow v. Commissioner *(1974) 416 U.S. 500, which holds that the objective of Sec. 174 is to provide an economic incentive for small businesses to engage in the search for development of new products.*

  (3) It is an error to disregard the prior rulings of this Court — such as (i) Louw, *TC Memo 1971-326; (ii)* Magee, *TC Memo 1973-211; (iii)* Kilroy, *TC Memo 1980-489; and (iv)* Kollsman, *TC Memo 1986-66 — that the qualifying*

expenditures need only be "proximately related" to an existing trade or business.

(4) It is an error to disregard respondent's own Regulation 1.174-2(a), Revenue Procedure 69-21, and Revenue Ruling 71-162 which treat the project development of technical software prototypes as noncapital expenditures.

Paragraph 5:—
  B. As to Issue II (Prototype Expenses)
    (1) In 1981, with the Economic Recovery Tax Act as the stimulus, petitioner (H) conceived a 25-volume tax book development project. The purpose of this project was the dual purpose of providing professional-level taxpayers with in-depth knowledge on one tax subject at a time, and for updating tax practitioners for their CPE (continuing professional education) requirements.

    (2) Petitioner envisioned a three-to-five-year development effort focusing on a 5-book pilot model. Prototype samples of the five titles were to be (and in fact were) printed and used for solicitation of commercial publishers. The samples were also used for critiquing by taxpayers, book review editors, and tax preparers. Most samples, however (due to their technical obsolescence), were destroyed.

    *(3) Petitioner relied on the phrase "in connection with" in Sec. 174(a) to expense his prototype samples and developmental supplies. Tax preparation, tax counseling, authoring of "tax related" articles for CPE units, and tax book development constitute a **reasonable nexus** between the developmental expenditures expensed and the trade or business of the taxpayer.*

    *(4) Petitioner's sole objective was to perfect a **pilot model** (on computer floppy disks) of five book titles. Each pilot model title would be the center title in each of five mini-series in a 25-volume project. Petitioner methodically explained the uncertainty and experimental nature of his effort to the examining agent who insisted that only Sec. 280 (capitalization) could apply.*

    (5) In 1976, Congress enacted Sec. 2119 of Public Law 94-455 which expressly prohibited the respondent from forcing capitalization procedures upon taxpayers for prototype samples and prepublication expenditures. Sec. 280 was repealed in 1986

and was replaced with Sec. 263A . . . which specifically excludes Sec. 174 expenditures.

Petition Example III

In the case of fraud, the burden of proof — supposedly — is on the IRS. The assignment of errors, therefore, need not be extensive. However, in the statement of facts, as many "affirmative defenses" as possible should be cited. This is to put the IRS firmly on notice that it is expected to prove its allegation.

Continuing with Tax Court Docket No. 8579-88, the following excerpts are presented:

Paragraph 4:—
   C. As to Issue III (Fraud Penalty)
      (1) It is an error to assert the fraud penalty as a coercive weapon to force the petitioner into accepting a position contrary to the clear legislative intent of Public Law 92-603 authorizing gifts and bequests to the Social Security Administration.
      (2) It is an error to assert the fraud penalty without itemizing the nine essential elements constituting fraudulent intent (prescribed by this and other Courts) and without carrying the burden of proof of "clear and convincing evidence" required by IRC Secs. 7214(a)(8) and 7454(a).

Paragraph 5:—
   C. As to Issue III (Fraud Penalty)
      (1) On June 13, 1984 at 9:30 a.m., before commencing TCMP examination of petitioner's 1981, 1982, and 1983 returns, respondent's agent, Ms. _____ said to petitioner—

   "We think you are trying to get away with something with the public gift of yours. Since you are a tax preparer, I'm here to warn you right now that we are going to level all of the penalties against you that we can think of."

She simply refused to recognize the 1972 gifts and bequests law; it was not implemented by any specifically-applicable IRS regulation. She then launched an exhaustive bank deposits analysis of petitioner's 1981, 1982, and 1983 income reportings. She found no underreporting of income (the primary requisite of fraud).

(2) On August 22, 1984 at 1:30 p.m., respondent's agent, Mr. _____, in the presence of respondent's agent, Ms. _____, said to petitioner—

> *"We think this whole public gift of yours is a fraud. We are going to assert the civil fraud penalty against you and turn it over to our Criminal Investigation Division."*

No basis other than his personal conjecture was given. Thereupon, Ms. _____ added—

> *"We can make it a lot easier on you, if you'll accept our position by applying for, collecting, and returning your Social Security benefits checks to the government."*

There is no such requirement designated by the 1972 Act nor by any regulation published by the respondent.

(3) On November 5, 1984 at 2:30 p.m., respondent's agent, Mr. _____ phoned petitioner to condemn him as follows—

> *"There was no such gift. Your whole idea is outrageous, preposterous, and frivolous. Section 170 doesn't apply here; it never did and it never will. I'm going to warn you right now: If you claim a charitable deduction for this on your 1984 return, I guarantee you I'll turn this over to our Criminal Investigation Division and recommend the 100% criminal fraud penalty in addition to the 50% civil fraud penalty."*

As a consequence of these threatening and coercive statements, petitioner did not claim his excess contributions carryover for 1984, as was his right, pursuant to Sec. 170(d)(1). Petitioner also continued making payments to the Social Security system thereby increasing substantially the valuation of his lifetime public gift.

(4) On November 20, 1984, petitioner made a written complaint to the President about the hostile and malicious attacks on the petitioner for his public gift (incidentally made at the suggestion of the President himself). This complaint was turned over to respondent's agent, Mr. _____, who, on November 30, 1984 wrote that—

"We do not, however, have sufficient resources to address the arguments of those individuals who have taken legal statements out of context in an effort to conclude that they are not subject to the tax laws."

Having insufficient resources to address an Act of Congress — the 1972 gifts and bequests authority — is not a legitimate basis for asserting the fraud penalty.

(5) On January 30, 1985, petitioner protested respondent's agent Mr. _____'s "30-day letter" saying, on page 5, that —

"The authorization of penalties was never intended as a means to intimidate and duress a taxpayer into accepting a position favorable to the IRS."

In documents accompanying petitioner's protest letter, at page 20 (re Issue III), petitioner referenced and cited portions of Public Law 92-603, Sec. 132(g), as implemented by 42 USC 401(i): Gifts and Bequests to the Social Security Administration. Thus, respondent's agents were well aware of this 1972 law. They simply refused to address it, thereby covering up dereliction of duty of the respondent. Such coverup is unlawful.

(6) Petitioner's public gift of his lifetime Social Security benefits involves an untested, unsettled, and possibly precedent-setting interpretation of the 1972 law. Constructive public policy could evolve, resulting in substantial savings to the U.S. Treasury. Respondent has cited no relevant authority whatsoever to support his fraud allegation. Nor has he cited any exact-issue court case which holds that such a gift constitutes fraudulent intent.

Answer Format & Contents

When the TC Clerk receives a petition, it is scanned for general form and content. It has to be typed or printed, on standard-size paper, with the notice of deficiency attached. If acceptable, the petition is stamped: ***Filed: U.S. Tax Court: (date).*** This information is entered on the official docket of the court, and a "Document Number" is assigned. On this point, TC Rule 35 says—

The docket number shall be placed by the parties on all papers thereafter filed in the case, and shall be referred to in all correspondence with the Court.

A stamped, docketed copy of the petition is served upon the Commissioner IRS by the TC Clerk. Rule 36 requires that the Commissioner file an answer to the petition. The form and content of the answer follows pretty much that of the petition itself. TC Rule 36(b), last sentence, says—

Paragraphs of the answer shall be designated to correspond to those of the petition to which they relate.

The idea behind requiring the IRS to answer every docketed petition is to fully advise the petitioner and the court of the nature of the IRS's defense. This is legal theory. In practice, the IRS's defense rests solely upon denying everything in your favor. Where it can't flat out deny it, it cites "lack of sufficient information" to admit or deny. It will then add that whatever law, regulation, or judicial ruling that you rely on is "irrelevant."

As to the responsive requirements for the IRS, TC Rule 36(b) says that—

It [the answer] *shall contain a specific admission or denial of each material allegation in the petition; however, if the Commissioner shall be without knowledge or information sufficient to form a belief as to the truth of an allegation, then the Commissioner shall so state, and such statement shall have the effect of a denial. . . . **In addition**, the answer shall contain a clear and concise statement of every ground, together with the facts in support thereof on which the Commissioner relies and has the burden of proof.* [Emphasis added.]

The "in addition" part of the above rule provides opportunity for the IRS to come up with additional assertions and allegations that it did not disclose in its notice of deficiency. In most cases, this is the real purpose of the answer. Otherwise, the IRS's "answers" to the petition provide no meaningful information whatever to the petitioner. Blanket denials are not meaningful information.

Your cue that the IRS is going to bring up additional allegations is when it requests extension of time to file its answer. Normally, the IRS has 60 days to answer a petition. Routinely, it requests 30-

to 60-day extensions thereto. And the court routinely grants the IRS its request.

The IRS has three years to make its case when auditing a return; it has six years — 2,190 days — when it asserts fraud. Yet, it still wants another 30 to 60 days to file its answer.

Answer Example I

We certainly want to illustrate for you how the IRS answers a petition. Our Example I relates to Issue I previously described. This issue, recall, has to do with the husband allegedly making a public gift of his lifetime Social Security benefits. The IRS answered that part of the petition in Paragraphs 4A(1) through (4) and 5A(1) through (6) as excerpted below:

4. Denies that respondent's determination contains any errors.

4A(1) — Admits that it would be an error to disregard the legislative intent of Public Law 92-603 but denies that the legislative intent, as claimed by petitioners, is relevant to the determination of petitioners' case.

4A(2) — Admits that it would be an error to disregard the judicial precedent of 38 TC 936 (1962) but denies that the judicial precedent, as claimed by petitioners, is relevant to the determination of petitioners' case.

4A(3) — Admits that it would be an error to disregard Revenue Ruling 82-169 but denies that said ruling, as claimed by petitioners, is relevant to the determination of petitioners' case.

4A(4) — Admits that it would be an error to disregard the valuation of petitioner's gift but denies that the valuation is applicable in the manner claimed by petitioners. Further alleges that petitioners have been advised how to make a gift of their Social Security benefits.

5A(1) — Denies that petitioner (H) paid money to the Social Security Administration for 28 years. Admits that [whatever] money was paid was accepted and credited.

5A(2) — Admits the first sentence. Admits the second sentence except alleges that the alleged entitlement to monthly payments is contingent upon the earnings of petitioner (H), and that entitlement is further contingent upon adherence to procedures by which such monthly payments are to be claimed.

5A(3) — Admits but alleges that the alleged quotation is only a partial representation of the statement made by the Chairman of the Senate Social Security Subcommittee.

5A(4) — Admits the first sentence. Denies for lack of information the second sentence. Admits the third sentence.

5A(5) — Denies for lack of sufficient information the first sentence. Denies the remaining allegations.

5A(6) — Denies the first sentence. Admits that the petitioner wrote a letter to the President but alleges that the President is not the individual authorized by 42 USC 401(i) to accept gifts and bequests made to the [Social Security Administration].

Answer Example II

Issue II, recall, comprises petitioner (H)'s expenditures for printing prototype samples (constituting a "pilot model") of a 25-volume tax book development project. As to the allegations in the petition, the IRS again denied that its determination contained any errors. It did, however, respond to each of the petitioners' Paragraphs 4B(1) through (4) and 5B(1) through (5). The excerpted passages follow:

4B(1) — Admits that it would be an error to disregard the legislative intent of IRC Sec. 174(a) but denies that the legislative intent, as claimed by petitioners, is relevant to the determination of petitioners' case.

4B(2) — Admits that it would be an error to disregard the ruling in Snow v. Commissioner 416 US 500 (1974) but denies that the judicial precedent is applicable in the manner claimed by petitioners.

4B(3) — Admits that it would be an error to disregard the rulings mentioned by petitioners but denies that the rulings are applicable in the manner claimed by petitioners.

4B(4) — Admits that it would be an error to disregard the Regulations, Revenue Procedures, and Revenue Rulings but denies that same are applicable to the determination of petitioners' case.

5B(1) — Admits the first and second sentences. Denies for lack of information the third sentence.

5B(2) — Denies for lack of sufficient information.

5B(3) — Denies for lack of sufficient information. Admits that there need only be a reasonable nexus between developmental expenditure and the trade or business of the petitioners but denies that such reasonable nexus existed in the petitioners' case. Denies the third sentence.
5B(4) — Denies for lack of sufficient information.
5B(5) — Admits the first sentence but alleges that the Public Law listed is inapplicable to the determination of the petitioners' case. Denies for lack of sufficient information the second and third sentences. Admits the fourth sentence but alleges that the allegations therein are irrelevant to the determination of this case.

Answer Example III

Issue III, recall, is the fraud penalty asserted separately against the husband and the wife. The notice of delinquency merely said that "all or part" of the petitioners' returns (1981, 1982, and 1983) constituted fraud. It is a glaring inequity of law that the IRS is not required to be more specific than this in its 90-day notice. Fortunately, a petition is one means for gaining more specifics than given in the notice. Again, however, as always, the IRS denies that it made any error.

In response to the petitioners' Paragraphs 4C(1) through (2) and 5C(1) through (6), the IRS plows through its "denial routine" again.

4C(1) — Denies that the fraud penalty has been asserted in an effort to coerce petitioners into accepting a position contrary to legislative intent.
4C(2) — Admits that respondent has the burden of proof with respect to the fraud penalty but denies that all elements of fraud need to be set forth.

5C(1) — Denies for lack of sufficient information the first sentence. Denies the second sentence. Admits the third sentence. Admits the fourth sentence but denies that under-reporting income is the primary requisite of fraud.
5C(2) — Denies for lack of sufficient information the first, second, and third sentences. Denies the fourth sentence.
5C(3) — Denies for lack of sufficient information.
5C(4) — Denies for lack of sufficient information the first and second sentences. Admits the third sentence but alleges that it is

not the basis for the assertion of the fraud penalty herein by respondent.
5C(5) — Admits the first, second, and third sentences. Denies the fourth and fifth sentences.
5C(6) — Denies the first and second sentences. Denies the third sentence except alleges that there is not a court case on point which holds that such a gift constitutes fraudulent intent. Admits that there is no willful intent to evade if a tax law is unsettled and a party reasonably relies thereon but denies that the petitioner reasonably relied.

After responding to Paragraphs 4 and 5 in the petition, the IRS then adds a catchall Paragraph 6, to wit:

Denies generally each and every allegation of the petition not hereinbefore specifically admitted, qualified, or denied.

Now, the "Further" Answer

All total, the IRS's answer to the taxpayers' petition consisted of 25 pages (8 1/2" x 11", typewritten). Of this number, 10 pages answered the petitioners' points; 15 pages raised new points and allegations relating to the IRS's contention of fraud. These new allegations were raised in three additional paragraphs, each beginning with—

FURTHER answering the petition . . .

The new allegations cited 67 — yes, 67 — fraudulent acts allegedly committed by the petitioner and his spouse. These 67 fraud allegations comprised approximately 2,300 words. Compare these 2,300 words with the 33-word allegation of fraud in the IRS's notice of deficiency. "What goes on here?" you ask.

When an agency of government alleges 67 acts of fraud (in 2,300 words) to justify its initial 33-word fraud allegation, something is drastically wrong.

Of course, it is all "legal." TC Rule 36(b) purposely allows the IRS to fabricate additional allegations on those matters for which it has the burden of proof. There is no limit to the number of allegations — be it 67 or 367 — that it can pose. Even if, later, it determines the IRS to be dead wrong, the Tax Court cannot discipline the IRS for its overzealousness and vindictiveness.

We are not going to recite to you the IRS's 67 fraud allegations. If you are really interested, you can contact the Clerk of the Tax Court. Request a copy of the IRS's Answer filed on or about August 19, 1988 (TC Docket No. 8579-88).

The gist of the 67 allegations of fraud is that petitioner (H) did not file an application to receive his Social Security benefits. For example, Paragraph 7(h)(31) of the IRS's Answer says—

> *As petitioner (H) did not apply for Social Security benefits, he was not entitled to receive such benefits.*

In other words, the IRS is saying that in order to make a public gift of one's lifetime Social Security benefits, he must apply for the benefits, receive them month-by-month, and gift them back to the government, month-by-month. For the instant case, that would mean over 200 (12 mo/yr x 16.8 yrs) separate public gifts! The petitioner did it in one fell swoop. And that's fraudulent?

In Paragraph 7(k) of its answer, the IRS exhumed an old dispute with petitioner (H) going back to his 1972-1976 self-employment tax years. This is an interesting issue in itself. But we'll let it unfold in the trial testimony in Chapter 9: Issue III. Could it be that a particular agent of the IRS was harboring a personal vendetta against the petitioner?

Two Examples in Reply

TC Rule 37 provides that a petitioner may file a Reply to that part of an answer which raises new allegations. The petitioner has 45 days to do so: no extensions. Even false allegations have to be responded to.

When you have an agency alleging 67 acts of fraud, you know that it will hound the court to deem all of its allegations admitted, unless you reply.

The reply to a **furthering** answer must respond to each and every allegation raised. TC Rule 37(b) says, in part—

> *In response to each material allegation in the answer and the facts in support thereof on which the Commissioner has the burden of proof, the reply shall contain a specific admission or denial.*

The petitioner prepared and timely filed an 11-page reply to the 67 fraud allegations. Obviously, we are not going to cite all of those responses here. We'll pick two examples, and then give you the synopsis of the reply.

For example, Paragraph 7(h)(31) posed by the IRS was cited verbatim above. The petitioner's response to that allegation was—

DENIED. "Application" (the right to receive benefits) and "entitlement" (the right to apply for them) are entirely different legal concepts. Petitioner (H)'s full legal rights to Social Security benefits vested in January 1981, regardless of whether he applied for them at that time or not. He attained "fully insured" status on that date [42 USC 414(a)]. Thereafter, except for his public gift, his right to apply became "inalienable."

Let's take the IRS's Paragraph 7(k), mentioned above, as another example. That was the matter of exhuming an old dispute: 1972-1976. In response, the petitioner replied as follows—

DENIED. This is another gross distortion of fact. That [prior] case is irrelevant, as no renunciation/gifting of lifetime Social Security benefits was involved. That 1976 case involved the proper filing of Form 4029: Application for Exemption from Tax on Self-Employment and Waiver of Benefits. It was based on conscientious objection to "double dipping" into the U.S. Treasury [as a military retiree and as a Social Security beneficiary].

Synopsis of Reply

Since the IRS can add "FURTHER" to its allegations, so, too, can the petitioner. Accordingly, in the synopsis portion of his reply, the petitioner added—

FURTHER, the petitioners, pursuant to Rule 39, allege as a special matter, that the respondent knowingly failed to timely implement Public Law 92-603 at Sec. 132(g) with specifically applicable published regulations, as was his duty, pursuant to 26 USC 7805(a); that such failure is the root cause of the principal issue herein; and that such failure has caused substantial damage and injury to petitioners. For this failure and his consequent and injury to petitioners. For this failure and his consequent unlawful acts, the respondent and each of his participating agents (pursuant to 26 USC 7344) are subject to punitive sanctions as prescribed in 26 USC 7214(a).

WHEREFORE, the petitioners pray that . . . sanctions be imposed on the respondent in the special pleading above.

As an editorial note, IRC Sections 7214 and 7344 address **Offences by Officers and Employees of the Treasury Department** . . . *when acting in connection with any revenue law of the United States.* Such persons . . . *shall be dismissed from office or discharged from employment* . . . [and] *fined not more than $10,000.*
The IRS can counter such accusations as the above with a Motion to Strike. TC Rule 52 says, in part, that—

Upon motion made by a party . . . within 30 days after service of a pleading, . . . the Court may order strike from the pleading any insufficient claim or defense . . . or scandalous matter.

Without stating its reasons, the court ordered that the sentence regarding offences by IRS officers and agents be stricken. Apparently said offences could be construed as "scandalous matter." And the Tax Court wants no part of any IRS scandal. The court allowed to stand, however, the petitioners' reliance on Public Law 92-603 at Sec. 132(g) [Gifts and Bequests to the Social Security Administration].

Actually, Three Petitions

You probably have the pleading picture well in mind by now. The disputed issues and counter issues get rather scrappy. In judicial parlance, the IRS's behavior is accepted as the "adversarial stance" for protecting the revenue of government.
This adversarial stance can cost the petitioner a lot of time, money, and attorney fees. During the pleading phase, many "papers" go back and forth between the petitioner, the Tax Court, and the IRS, and between the attorneys of the parties involved. For instructional effect, we depict these numerous filings and servings in Figure 4.3. Not only does the taxpayer/petitioner have to pay taxes to support the IRS and its entourage of attorneys, he has to pay for

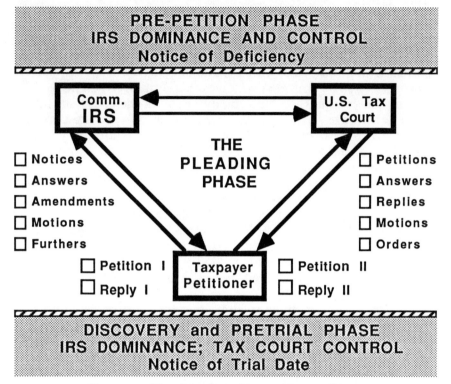

Fig. 4.3 - The Pleading Phase "Paper Mill"

his own support and that of his attorney as well. The IRS can file and serve tons of pleading papers without great concern for out-of-pocket costs.

To keep the Figure 4.3 paper mill churning, the IRS was in a position to force the petitioners to file a *second* petition with the Tax Court. This was for years 1985 and 1986. This required a repetition of "all of the above."

Because a different set of IRS auditors was involved in the 1985-1986 returns, no fraud penalty was asserted initially. The petitioner prepared his Petition II accordingly. The IRS answered. It immediately followed its initial answer with an amended answer alleging the same 67 "points of fraud" as in its Answer I. The cumulative total now came to 134 allegations of fraud. Bear in mind that the IRS has to prove ONLY ONE of these 134 allegations. If it does, the court can sustain the fraud penalty against the petitioner for all six years!

Obviously, we are not going to rehash Petition II and its pleading papers. We just want you to be aware that there were two complete petition cycles on the same disputive issues I, II, and III. There was also a complete petition cycle (Petition III) on Issue IV.

In case you question the veracity of any of the above statements (or any of those in the chapters which follow), you are cordially invited to request copies of any of the papers of interest to you from the Clerk of the U.S. Tax Court. For identification purposes, the three petitions (and all papers) are docketed as:

Petition I — Docket No. 8579-88
Endorsed, filed April 28, 1988
Petition II — Docket No. 28098-88
Endorsed, filed October 27, 1988
Petition III — Docket No. 3952-93
Endorsed, filed February 25, 1993

It should be self-evident from what we have revealed thus far that going into Tax Court is not for the weak of heart. One has to believe resoundingly in his position. He has to be prepared to pay the price. The "price" is not only in terms of dollars, but in terms of time, aggravation, frustration, and — yes — disenchantment with government and its revenue system. Included in the disenchantment is disrespect for the IRS.

5

DISCOVERY & PRETRIAL

"Discovery" Starts With A Pretrial Order Enabling The IRS To Build Its Case, After Just Saying "No" (And Sitting On Its Thumbs) For 5 Years Or More. It Inundates The Petitioner With Requests For DOCUMENTS AND THINGS (Rule 72), Admissions (Rule 90), Stipulations (Rule 91), And Motions To Compel. The Discovery Rules Are Of Little Benefit To A Petitioner, As The IRS Is Allowed To Secrete Evidence It Intends To Use For Impeachment. No IRS Agent Or Official Ever Signs "Under Penalties Of Perjury." For This Reason, BEWARE OF Entering Into Joint Stipulations With The IRS.

Comes now the second paper-mill phase of your venture into Tax Court. This is the discovery and pretrial phase. The purpose of this phase is to gather documentary evidence and witnesses, and organize and preview them for presentation at trial. The arena of discovery is supposed to be by informal conferences, consultations, and communications between the parties. It is *supposed to be* a two-way cooperative affair: exchanging of documents, information . . . and so on.

When dealing with the IRS, most all of the discovery procedures are a one-way affair. You cooperate with them, they stonewall any cooperation with you.

Primarily, discovery is a process by which the IRS inundates the petitioner (and his/her attorney) with endless demands for documents, admissions, and concessions. This effort is particularly abhorrent where the IRS has the burden of proof, as in the case of fraud. It picks a target year, such as 1981 in the case here, and demands all the petitioner's documents from six years before . . . and six years after. It essentially tries to reaudit those returns all over again.

There is a strategy behind the IRS discovery efforts. One, it is to keep the petitioner confused with endless paper actions, always mindful that the petitioner has to pay for the legal services to respond. Two, it is to distract the petitioner from preparing his own case objectively. And, three, there is the likely chance the petitioner and/or his counsel will trip up on some material item that is sufficient cause for dismissing the case.

Accordingly, in this chapter, we want to discuss the standing pretrial order: its purpose and contents. We also want to familiarize you with the primary discovery rules — 72, 90, and 91 — which the IRS will use to the fullest. In the process, we want to alert you to certain dirty tricks of the IRS. Although your accuser and adversary is the Commissioner of Internal Revenue, he NEVER, EVER has to appear at trial.

The Pretrial Order

Discovery officially begins when each party to the dispute receives a Standing Pretrial Order signed by the Tax Court judge (called: *trial judge*) assigned to the case. This order is issued approximately 30 days after the petitioner's Reply is filed with the court in Washington, D.C. The order sets the trial date, and is headed: NOTICE SETTING CASE FOR TRIAL.

Regarding Issues I, II, III, and IV that we are going to use for illustration purposes, *three* pretrial orders were promulgated. For the moment, we'll differentiate them as Pretrial I, Pretrial II, and Pretrial III. For authenticity purposes, the actual dates were:

Pretrial I   —   Docket No. 8579-88
                        Date of Notice: 10-07-88
                        Date of Trial: **3-13-89**
Pretrial II   —   Docket No. 28098-88
                        Date of Notice: 6-27-89
                        Date of Trial: **12-04-89**
Pretrial III   —   Docket No. 3952-93
                        Date of Notice: 11-26-93
                        Date of Trial: **2-18-94**

Note that two of the trial dates were set approximately nine months apart. Experiences from the first pretrial proceedings were beneficial in the second pretrial proceedings.

From this point on, however, we are going to "blend" the three pretrial orders, and give a composite discussion and example of the discovery process.

The key paragraph in the notice accompanying a pretrial order reads in full as—

Your attention is called to the Court's requirement that, if the case cannot be settled on a mutually satisfactory basis, the parties, before trial, must agree in writing to all facts and all documents about which there should be no disagreement. Therefore, the parties should contact each other promptly and cooperate fully so that the necessary steps can be taken to comply with this requirement. YOUR FAILURE TO COOPERATE MAY ALSO RESULT IN DISMISSAL OF THE CASE AND ENTRY OF DECISION AGAINST YOU.

We are aware of no case which has been dismissed due to the IRS's failure to cooperate. Many cases have been dismissed due to the petitioner's failure (as alleged by the IRS). This does not mean that the IRS cooperates; it simply means that the IRS gets away with its noncooperation. It has more practice at this than petitioners do.

Herein lies the great danger — and the seedbed of IRS abuses — in the discovery process. Do be patient; we offer specific examples below.

Standing Order Contents

The standing order signed by the trial judge is a two-page document. It consists of approximately 800 words. It is arranged in two parts: Policies and Requirements, with unnumbered paragraphs in each part.

We believe that this unnumbering of the paragraphs in an 800-word court document is the first weak link in the discovery process. It allows the IRS to select any set of words and phrases, without reference to a particular paragraph, to badger the petitioner(s) into submission and concessions.

Unnumbered though they may be, there are four distinct policy statements in the standing order. The leadoff phrases to each of these statements are—

1. You are expected to begin discussions . . .
2. If difficulties are encountered . . .
3. Continuances will be granted only in exceptional cases . . .
4. If any unexcused failure to comply with this Order . . .

The idea behind these policy statements is, in the event of "communication difficulties" between the parties, to encourage telephone conferences between the opposing counsel and the trial judge. This requires contacting the judge and opposing party simultaneously. The Pretrial Order provides the phone number for this. Obviously, the number of such conference calls should be kept to a minimum.

In the Requirement part of the standing order, there are six paragraphs (also unnumbered). Each paragraph is a separate self-contained Order in itself. The lead-in sentence to all six orders reads, in part—

To effectuate the foregoing policies . . ., it is hereby
ORDERED that—

Obviously, there is not space here to cite all six orders verbatim. Instead, we characterize them in Figure 5.1 with highly abbreviated phrases. The abbreviations can be used for indexing purposes later. We want to show that, even in a court order (albeit pretrial), the IRS can and does abuse its privilege as a tax-supported government agency.

Unfortunately, the discovery process authorized by the Figure 5.1 standing order is dominated by the IRS. This is because the IRS attorney (or attorneys) assigned to a petitioner's case has no overhead to pay, has unlimited staff at his disposal, and has access to computer-stored tax, financial, and inter-governmental information on every petitioner.

The only recourse that a petitioner has to thwart this IRS dominance is TC Rule 101(e): Jurisdiction. This subrule reads in essential part—

Nothing contained in this Rule [relating to sanctions and discipline of counsel] *shall be construed to deny the Court such powers as are necessary for the Court to* **maintain control** *over proceedings conducted before it.* [Emphasis added.]

UNITED STATES TAX COURT
WASHINGTON, D.C. 20217

STANDING PRETRIAL ORDER	
Part A	**POLICIES**

1. Begin discussions ....
2. If difficulties ....
3. Continuances: Only if exceptional ....
4. Unexcused failure to comply ....

Part B	**REQUIREMENTS**
ORDER 1	Re Documentary and Written Evidence
ORDER 2	Re Trial Memorandum (15 days before trial)
ORDER 3	Re Identification and Testimony of Witnesses
ORDER 4	Re Settlement Procedures (if reached before trial)
ORDER 5	Re Readiness for Trial
ORDER 6	Re Mutual Exchange of Documents

Washington, D.C.

Dated: _____(date)_____   _____/s/_____
                                    Trial Judge

Fig. 5.1 - Highly Abbreviated Contents of Pretrial Order

Thus, although the IRS dominates the pretrial proceedings, the TC trial judge has the final say and control.

Order 1: Loophole for IRS

Order 1 in Figure 5.1 is the longest single paragraph in the 2-page standing order of the court. It consists of approximately 165 words. The general idea behind this order is that the parties "fully cooperate" in preparing and organizing those documents that they intend to use as evidence at trial. The documents are to be "exchanged by the parties" at least 15 days before trial. But the order provides a loophole for the IRS when it asserts fraud. Let us explain.

For you to see the loophole, we need to quote pertinent portions from the order itself. The relevant words and phrases are—

*ORDERED that . . . All documentary and written evidence shall be marked and stipulated in accordance with Rule 91(b), **unless** the evidence is to be **used to impeach** the credibility of a witness. . . . Any documents or materials which **a party** expects to utilize in the event of trial (**except for impeachment**), . . . shall be identified in writing and exchanged by the parties at least 15 days before the first day of the trial session.* [Emphasis added.]

If you reread this order, there is ambiguity with respect to the extent of secretiveness of impeachment documents. First of all, this protection is afforded only to the IRS. Yes, the order says "a party," but how does a petitioner impeach (discredit the testimony of) the Commissioner of IRS? Such a respondent (or any direct delegate) NEVER appears at trial. How can you charge the Commissioner or anyone else in the IRS with fraud under the TC redetermination rules? You can't. And, even if you could, the defense would be "sovereign immunity."

Thus, the IRS is left to its own devices for interpreting the impeachment exception of Order 1 any way it wants. Its interpretation is that, if there is one document to be used for impeachment purposes in a stack of 100 documents, the entire 100-document stack can be secreted, and the 15-day exchange rule does not apply. In a fraud case, discrediting a petitioner with one or more impeachment documents is the name of the game.

Because of this ambiguity in Order 1, the Tax Court — perhaps unwittingly — is aiding and abetting the IRS in its dirty tricks game. Now you know why the IRS can fabricate 134 allegations of fraud (over six years) and not have to reveal to the petitioner(s) or counsel the documentary basis of its allegations.

Rule 72 Re Documents

For tax disputes, the most commonly used discovery rule is TC Rule 72: **Production of Documents and Things.** This heading alone should send a message to you. How do you get the IRS to produce its "documents and things"? It is protected by sovereign immunity, privileged information, and internal work product rules. Here, again, in reality, the IRS is favored.

It is practically impossible for a petitioner to gain access to the same documentary evidence that the IRS has access to. Although the discovery rules apply to "any party," the party most frequently using the rule is the IRS. Discovery is the right to access any information which is not privileged and which is relevant to the subject matter in the pending case. When the IRS asserts fraud, its scope of discovery is virtually unlimited.

In this unlimited vein, Rule 72(a) states in part that—

Any party may . . . serve on the other party a request to: (1) Produce . . . any designated documents (including writings, drawings, graphs, charts, photographs, phono-records, and other data from which information can be obtained . . .) or to inspect and copy . . . any of the foregoing items. . . .
(2) Permit entry upon designated . . . property . . . for the purpose of inspection and measuring . . . or sampling . . . any designated object or operation thereon.

Even if the IRS's repeated requests for documents are unduly burdensome and expensive, any objections by the petitioner are almost invariably denied by the court (especially when allegations of fraud comprise one of the issues). This counterweighs against the wording of Rule 72(b) which says, in part—

The party upon whom the request is served . . . shall state, with respect to each item or category, that inspection and related activities will be permitted as requested, unless the request is objected to in whole or part, in which event the reason for objection shall be stated.

Without going through all of the nitty-gritty of IRS documentary demands, petitioner objections, IRS motions to compel, IRS requests for admissions, and further IRS motions to compel, we present in Figure 5.2 a schematic summary of the IRS discovery behavior regarding Issues I, II, and III previously described.

Discovery is supposed to be completed 45 days before trial begins [Rule 70(a)(2)], but rarely does the Tax Court enforce this rule against the IRS. As a result, the IRS keeps pushing for you to disclose your information to it, but it secretes its information from you . . . until "10 seconds" before trial. We mean **10 seconds** literally. When the court reporter announces: "All rise," as the TC judge opens the door from his/her chambers, the IRS then shoves its pile of exhibits towards the petitioner or his counsel.

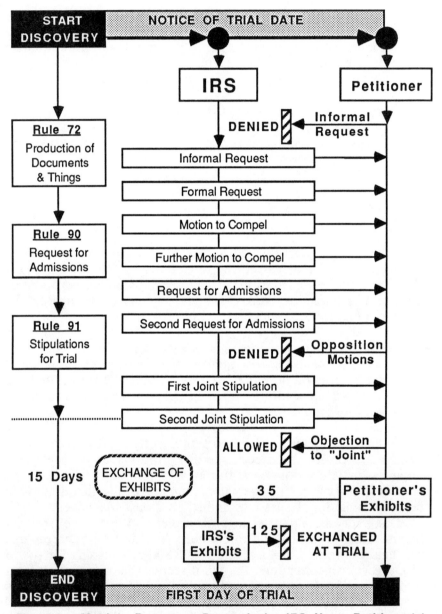

Fig. 5.2 - Multiple Document Demands by IRS Upon Petitioner(s)

IRS "Shuffles" Your Documents

There is reason why the IRS waits until 10 seconds before the TC judge enters the courtroom to exchange documents. It has "shuffled" those documents furnished to it by the petitioner or his counsel. Documents which are obviously helpful to the petitioner are surreptitiously rearranged by the IRS attorney representing the Commissioner-in-absentia.

Sensing this rearrangement — called *shuffling* — the petitioner or his attorney is left fumbling and scurrying, trying to resurrect the documents for orderly presentation as evidence. When the petitioner's attorney starts objecting (as the trial opens) and turns to scold the IRS, the IRS attorney refuses to respond. The IRS attorney in a smart-alecky fashion directs that all attorney-to-attorney communications be conducted through the presiding judge. The judge hasn't seen the documents, so he/she does not know what the fuss is all about. We cite in the next chapter an actual three-way courtroom verbal exchange over the document shuffling problem.

Once you catch on that the IRS has shuffled your documents to your detriment, you'll understand why the Figure 5.2 multitude of discovery demands were made upon you. The IRS demands keep you off guard and disorganized. You are overwhelmed with paper.

At the bottom of Figure 5.2, we show the number of documents intended to be used as evidence by each party (for Issues I, II, and III). The petitioner submitted 35 documents which totaled approximately 50 sheets of paper. The IRS submitted 125 documents which totaled approximately 2,500 separate sheets of paper! The IRS documents, all of which came from the petitioner or from his tax files in IRS hands, comprised a stack of paper nearly 18 inches high!

When you are confronted in the presence of a TC judge with 125 marked documents consisting of 2,500 sheets of paper, intentional shuffling by the IRS gives the natural appearance of an ordinary human mixup. Since the judge is not going to sort matters out, the IRS gets away with its despicable game.

From our experience with the IRS, we can identify at least eight variant shuffling techniques that the IRS uses against petitioners. Because these matters so easily escape the attention of the unwary, we present them in tabulated form in Figure 5.3. The techniques work only when there is a massive number of papers to be examined in open court. In an adversarial situation, such as a tax dispute,

Massive "Stack" of Documentary Evidence }		Over 900 sheets of paper Over 6 inches in height	
Item	Technique	Description	Effect on Petitioner
1	Needle-in-haystack	Key petitioner documents randomly interspersed; no record of whereabouts.	Key evidence becomes virtually lost; court gets exasperated.
2	Piggy-backing	Tacked on to a well marked (but unrelated) document.	Must unscramble and apologize to court for misidentity.
3	Back-to-back	Continuation of strategic matter onto back side, in multiple pages of one-sides.	Makes document incomplete, thereby weakening its impact on the court.
4	Cross-year substitution	Similar subject document and form, but years "crossed".	Adds to confusion; requires hasty resorting, explanation.
5	Sequential pages un-numbered	First page well marked, but subsequent pages (same document) unnumbered.	Forces delay; requires oral clarification as to specific page referenced.
6	Copy machine "problem"	Properly marked and in proper order, but photocopy intentionally illegible.	Causes misreading and "stumbling"; key data made unintelligible.
7	The "sneak-in"	Irrelevant (but damaging) matter inserted surreptitiously in the stack.	Becomes part of the "stipulated evidence" without petitioner's knowledge.
8	Unrelated "batching"	Sequentially marked, but unrelated subject matters "bunched together".	Confuses the judge, who tends to look only at top page subject matter.

Fig. 5.3 - Various Shuffling Techniques Used by IRS

who has the time, money, and power to amass a mountain of legal papers other than the IRS? So, be forewarned.

When we get to some of the trial testimony in Chapters 7 through 10, you'll see that even the TC judge gets confused. Confused TC judges tend to give the benefit of any doubt to the IRS: seldom to the petitioner. This comes under the "presumption of correctness" theory which protects the IRS.

Setting the Perjury Trap

Have you ever noticed that, when signing a tax return (Form 1040), there's a perjury clause that you are signing? On the 1040, above your signature, it reads—

Under penalties of perjury, I declare that I have examined this return and accompanying schedules and statements, and to the best of my knowledge and belief, they are true, correct, and complete.

Similar wording appears on other specialized tax forms and applications, which may or may not attach directly to Form 1040. In all tax form cases, the perjury clause is in fine print. It is seldom read and digested. This is because it has little practical significance in routine tax affairs.

Only when there is a tax dispute in a judicial setting — such as in Tax Court or other federal court — does the perjury clause carry weight.

Never does any IRS agent or official sign any perjury clause. So, the "perjury trap" can only be set against taxpayers: never against the IRS or its Commissioner-in-absentia.

The perjury trap does not have to be set for the year (or years) in which the tax dispute arises. It can be set for **any year** prior to the trial date. Consequently, the IRS's entrapment procedure is to pick some prior (though unrelated) year in which some error was found on the face of the form on which the perjury clause appears. It then confronts the taxpayer with this prior-year error at trial, when his memory recall is focusing on the at-issue years. While perjuring oneself on an out-of-the-blue unrelated matter is not fatal to the tax year at issue, it embarrasses the petitioner and can put him in an unfavorable light with the trial judge.

Any form of perjury frameup is "open game" when fraud is asserted by the IRS (such as Issue III). In this illustrative case, the perjury trap was **Form 4029**: Application for Exemption from Tax on Self-Employment Income and Waiver of Benefits. It was signed in 1974 "under penalties of perjury" for tax year 1972. It listed the applicant's religious affiliation as the Universal Life Church. This form became the subject of litigation in a Federal District Court which went to trial in December, 1976. This was well before the Tax Court at-issue years of 1981, etc.

Nevertheless, there was no forewarning to the petitioner or his counsel that a 1972 tax matter was going to be raised by the IRS in a 1981 tax dispute, to be heard in Tax Court in 1989.

In retrospect, the probable forewarning came in the form of the IRS's request for admissions. It appears to have been item 11 in a listing of 20 items. The entrapment item read—

Item 11 - [Petitioner] *was ordered by a Federal District Court in 1976 to pay Social Security withholding taxes.* [Petitioner] *previously objected . . . for religious reasons as a member of the Universal Life Church.*

Petitioner's answer to this request for admission was—

Item 11 - *This request is objected to on the basis that it has no subject matter relevancy to the issue of this Tax Court Petition.*

As you'll see in Chapter 9, the above item 11 became the cornerstone of the IRS's allegation of fraud (Issue III). Why the Tax Court allowed this item as evidence is one of those mysterious favoritisms the TC has towards the IRS.

Rule 90 Re Admissions

TC Rule 90: Requests for Admission, is one of the longest rules of all. It consists of approximately 1,500 words. Like most TC rules, it starts out with the phrase: *A party may . . .* As with most TC discovery rules, the party which uses the rules most is the IRS. It has the time, money, staff, and access to the entire federal government's sources of information. And since no government agent or official ever signs anything under "penalties of perjury," a petitioner's request for admissions to the IRS are categorically denied. No denial explanation by the IRS need by given.

Rule 90 is the technique by which the IRS can hypothesize a scenario of facts and circumstances, and force a petitioner to either admit, deny, or object to them. Rule 90(c) instructs that if the petitioner does not respond within 30 days, the hypothetical facts are deemed admitted. They are then admissible as evidence against the petitioner.

Rule 90(c) goes on to further state that—

Each matter is deemed admitted unless . . . the party to whom the request is directed [the petitioner] **serves upon the requesting party** [the IRS] *(1) a written answer specifically admitting or denying the matter involved in whole or part . . ., or (2) an objection,* **stating in detail** *the reasons therefor. . . . A denial shall fairly meet the substance of the requested admission, and, when good faith requires that a party qualify an answer or deny only a part of a matter, such party* [the petitioner] **shall specify so much of it as is true and deny or qualify the remainder.** [Emphasis added.]

Rule 90(c) places quite a denial burden on the petitioner. It means that the IRS can "twist" and distort a fact out of context, with impunity. This puts the petitioner in the position of having to unravel the twistings, explain the part which is true, and deny the part or innuendo which is untrue.

Can't you see the potential for abuse? For example, the IRS can assert that the petitioner did — or did not — do a specific act in a specific year. The act may be correct, but the year may be wrong. Or, the year may be correct, and the act wrong. Or, the act may be part true and part untrue. There is no requirement that the IRS police itself in its honesty of stated facts. The entire burden of correcting the IRS is on the petitioner.

Rule 90(f): Effect of Admission, goes on to say that—

Any matter admitted under this Rule is **conclusively established** *unless the Court* **on motion** *permits withdrawal or modification of the admission.* [Emphasis added.]

This subrule means that if a petitioner later discovers that he has been duped by the IRS, he has to make a formal motion to the court. The motion must detail the merits of one's oversight.

Rule 91 Re Stipulations

TC Rule 91: Stipulations for Trial, is another approximately 1,500-word rule. In essence, it requires that both parties — the IRS as well as the petitioner — stipulate (agree) to as much as possible of the evidentiary documents and facts as is reasonable and fair between the parties. The purpose of this, of course, is to save the court's time and permit it to focus more closely on the controversial issues. All matters that can be agreed upon before trial become part of the trial evidence for consideration by the TC judge at time of his/her decision.

On the surface at least, Rule 91 puts the parties more nearly on parity than Rules 72 (re Documents) and 90 (re Admissions). However, Rule 91 is quite extensive . . . and demanding. It is not a matter of discovery options between the parties; it is a mandate of the court.

The gist of the stipulations mandate is found in subrule 91(a)—

> *The parties **are required** to stipulate, to the fullest extent to which complete or qualified agreement can or fairly should be reached, . . . **regardless** of whether such matters involve fact or opinion or the application of law to fact. Included . . . are all facts, all documents and papers or contents or aspects thereof, and **all evidence** which fairly should not be in dispute. When the **truth or authenticity** of facts or evidence claimed to be relevant by one party is not disputed, an objection on the ground of materiality or relevance may be noted by the other party but is not to be regarded as just cause for refusal to stipulate. . . . The fact that any matter may have been obtained through discovery or requests for admissions or through any other authorized procedure is **not grounds for omitting** such matter from the stipulation.* [Emphasis added.]

There are other mandatory elements of Rule 91, but it is best that we digest them for you in Figure 5.4. Because of its many mandatory elements, the IRS uses Rule 91 as a club to browbeat petitioners and their counsel into virtually conceding the core issue(s) of a case. Always keep in mind that the IRS has more experience with the TC rules — and knows what it can get away with — than individual petitioners or their legal counsel.

Rule 91(d): Objections, may be invoked at commencement of trial or for good cause shown during trial. This is what the rule says. But, in reality, the IRS treats any objection to its stipulations as "noncompliance" with Rule 91. It thereby seeks the court's approval to *compel* a petitioner to enter into stipulations with it. [Rule 91f(1).]

Beware of Joint Stipulations

There are grave dangers when stipulating to anything jointly with the IRS. Although the IRS strives to create the impression that

Rule 91	STIPULATIONS FOR TRIAL	
Subrule	Heading	Synopsis of Contents
91 (a)	Stipulations Required	To the "fullest extent"
(a) (1)	General....................	All documents, papers, facts, and evidence which should not be fairly in dispute.
(a) (2)	Comprehensive........	Be set forth comprehensively in logical order of relevance, irrespective of mode of discovery.
91 (b)	Form......................	Clear and concise with annexed documents appropriately lettered or numbered.
91 (c)	Filing.....................	At or before commencement of trial. Need not be offered separately as evidence.
91 (d)	Objections..............	To be noted in the stipulation or at commencement of trial. Must expressly identify.
91 (e)	Binding Effect.........	Treated as "conclusive admissions" without qualifications or change.
91 (f)	Noncompliance	By either party
(f) (1)	Motion to Compel......	Not later than 45 days prior to trial, showing "with particularity" the item of concern.
(f) (2)	Procedure................	Order to Show Cause served. Must be responded to within 20 days, with proof of service.
(f) (3)	Failure of Response...	The proposed stipulation will be ordered admitted. Evasive responses disregarded.
(f) (4)	Matters Considered...	Genuinely controverted or doubtful issues of fact ought not be stipulated.

Fig. 5.4 - Synopsis of Mandatory Contents : TC Rule 91

only joint stipulations are allowed, such is not so. True, the TC court prefers joint stipulations (saves paper and time), but there is no requirement to this effect.

The problem with joint stipulations is the credibility of the IRS. So often it will solicit oral agreement to generally understood facts and documents, then it will prepare the written stipulations to its own advantage. It may even include untrue statements which it knows are untrue. It may dishevel (disarrange) uncontroverted documents, such as tax returns, and will omit attachments, schedules, and relevant computations..

To illustrate this reprehensible behavior of the IRS, we present excerpts from a letter written by the petitioner's counsel to the IRS. The letter was written between Trial I (March 1989) and Trial II (December 1989) with respect to Issues I, II, and III previously mentioned. The letter read, in extracted part—

Dear Mr._____ [IRS attorney]:

I received your proposed joint stipulation on October 23, 1989. I am both discouraged and disappointed.

I am discouraged because you continue to ignore our conversations and agreements.

I am disappointed because you have already proven to me that you are not above misleading me to your own advantage, and you continue to insult my intelligence with more attempts to mislead me.

Yet, you propose this stipulation that attempts to get me to stipulate to 127 exhibits. You added a sentence, that unless I object to each and every one of these exhibits as evidence, in my opening statement at trial, such exhibit would be admitted. You ignored the agreement we made in our telephone conference with the judge [for Trial II].

Many of your 127 paragraphs are simply untrue or incorrect. Many have nothing to do with, nor in any way are in compliance with, our conference call with the judge [for Trial II].

Finally, I am going to ask that you never insult my intelligence again!

_____/s/_____
Petitioner's Attorney

The above excerpts point out that the IRS will not only ignore its "gentlemen's agreements" with petitioners and/or petitioners' counsel, but will also ignore any telephone agreements made with the assigned trial judge.

Here's an actual example of how the IRS wrote its proposed joint stipulation 30—

Petitioner (H) saved $1739 in self-employment tax for 1981 as a result of claiming exempt status.

First of all, the petitioner **lost** $439 per month or $5,268 per year of Social Security benefits by his renunciatory effort. Secondly, he never claimed "exempt status"; he claimed a charitable contribution for his public gift. And, thirdly, the petitioner paid the 1981 self-employment tax (and all years subsequent thereto) before trial. This jumped his monthly entitlements to $1,079 from $439. All of this was made known to the IRS attorney **before** he wrote the above stipulation.

Authenticity versus Admissibility

A major bone of contention in stipulatory practices with the IRS is the issue of "authenticity versus admissibility." The IRS tries to get the petitioner or his counsel to authenticate a document, then treats the authentication as unchallengeable admissibility of that document at trial. The IRS then reserves unto itself the right to rebut or corroborate the stipulated document with additional evidence which it has secreted.

To "authenticate" means to establish the genuineness of a document as presented. That is, the document is reviewed to see if it has been falsified or doctored in any way. A document may be authenticated for stipulation purposes, **without** agreeing that it is automatically admissible as evidence at trial.

Do not hastily authenticate any document that the IRS stipulates, without first carefully reviewing that document. The IRS is not above falsification by disarranging and/or omitting pages. For example, one of the stipulatory documents the IRS had proposed re Issues I, II, and III was the petitioners' 1981 tax return. On its surface, this was a reasonable stipulatory item. But when the IRS's photocopied version of the 1981 return was examined, there were flagrant disarrangements and omissions. Schedule A (for Issue I), Schedule C (for Issue II), and Schedule SE (for Issue III) were upside down, out of order, and partially illegible. Three other important attachments (letters to President, Congressman, and Social Security) were omitted.

The typical (official) stipulatory wording that the IRS proposes is—

*The parties stipulate to the authenticity **and admissibility** for any purpose of the exhibits identified as joint exhibits, subject to objection for relevancy. Any relevancy objection may be made with respect to all or any part of the stipulation at time of offering into evidence, but **all other evidentiary objections are waived** unless specifically expressed with this Stipulation.* [Emphasis added.]

Evidentiary objections to stipulated documents SHOULD NEVER BE WAIVED . . . by either party. The IRS knows this. This is why it carries out for itself its stipulation escape hatch, namely:

The truth of assertions within Stipulated Exhibits may be rebutted or corroborated by additional evidence [by the IRS].

The above-board way to stipulate exhibits is the wording used by the petitioners' counsel, to wit—

The parties agree that the following exhibits to be offered into evidence are authentic electronic reproductions of the originals and can be treated as if they are originals. The description of each exhibit is for reference convenience of the court and is to have no evidentiary or legal impact.

In a nutshell, you cannot trust the IRS to be honest and above-board in its stipulatory transactions. This is a sad and disturbing realization after some 80+ years of the IRS's history. Because so few taxpayers (relatively) go into Tax Court, the IRS gets away with its misbehaviors.

6

TRIAL PROCEDURE

> **The Petitioner And The IRS Each Prepares A Trial Memorandum Outlining Its Portrayal Of The Issues, With Its Witnesses And Evidence. It Is The Petitioner Who "Moves The Trial Along." Doing So, He Must First Destroy The PRESUMPTION Of Correctness That The IRS Enjoys. The Petitioner's Burden Of Proof Is Carried Only When He Establishes An ERROR OF SUBSTANCE In The IRS's "Determination" Of Tax And Penalties. Once An Error Is Shown, The IRS Shifts To Other Tax And Legal Theories To Destroy The Creditability Of The Petitioner. A Permanent Transcript Of The Trial Is Prepared.**

Trial does not officially begin until the assigned judge enters the assigned Tax Courtroom in the assigned Federal Building in the designated city and state, at or about the designated hour, on or about the designated date . . . and sits himself/herself down at the judge's podium.

Trial "starts to begin" the moment the TC judge opens the door from his/her office chambers (adjacent to the courtroom). At that moment, the court stenographer (clerk) announces: "All rise, please." After the judge steps up to the podium and sits down, the clerk announces:

All be seated. The court is now in session.

In some cases, the TC judge himself/herself will address those persons present: "Be seated, ladies and gentlemen." After all in the courtroom are seated, the judge will address the clerk:

Will you call the case that we have for trial?

To which the clerk responds by announcing the docket number of the case and the name(s) of the petitioner(s).

The clerk then addresses the petitioner(s) or his/her/their counsel and the IRS attorney representing the Commissioner-in-absentia, saying—

Please state your appearance for the record.

At this moment, trial begins.

The time between the judge opening the door from his/her chambers and the clerk addressing the attorneys to state their appearance spans approximately 10 to 20 seconds. This is the time when the IRS attorney shoves his pile of papers and documents in front of the petitioners' attorney. This is in full compliance with the AT-OR-BEFORE-commencement-of-trial requirement for exchanging documents and things between the parties.

Other than controversial procedural matters — of which the "10- to 20-second exchange" is one — we focus in this chapter on the purely procedural aspects of any Tax Court trial. Knowing these procedural aspects is the first step in understanding why the IRS behaves pretrial the way it does. The purpose of Tax Court is to **redetermine** the amount of tax (and penalty) in dispute. It is not to question the motives or behavior of the IRS.

Trial Memorandums

With but one exception, all Tax Court judges step to the podium with an open mind. Although each judge has his or her own human frailties, each is a genuinely conscientious person with no preconceived bias against either party. Although, as you'll see below, there are procedural biases favoring the IRS, there are no decisional biases at the outset. This is because, as specialists in tax law, the duties of a TC judge require the withholding of final judgment until all of the disputed facts and evidence are in.

The exception to this open mind of a TC judge is the Trial Memorandum. Not less than 15 days before trial, each party must submit *directly to the judge* its version of the tax issues in dispute and why. Thus, there are two separate memorandums: one by the petitioner, one by the IRS.

Technically, the opposing parties are supposed to exchange their trial memorandums between each other, also not less than 15 days before trial. Seldom does the IRS do this. It has "impeachment rights," if you recall. It wants to catch the petitioner and his counsel by surprise. Consequently, the IRS's trial memorandum is another one of those "documents and things" shoved at the petitioner in that 10-second trial frame above.

The purpose of a trial memorandum by each party is to acquaint the judge with the core particulars of each tax dispute. Submitting each memorandum 15 days before trial allows the judge time to review the applicable tax law(s) on which each party relies. Other matters, such as synopsis of the facts, expected testimony of witnesses, and stipulatory documents, are also included in each memorandum. The trial judge will almost certainly at least skim-read personally each party's memorandum.

Rarely does a trial judge review the mountains of papers — petitions, answers, replies, requests, admissions, motions, procedural controversies, etc. — filed with the Chief Clerk of the Tax Court. There is a legitimate reason for this disregard. A TC judge's disregard of all these papers is based on the *de novo* theory of TC procedures. ["De novo" means: once more, again, anew.] The judge wants to rule on the admissibility of evidence on his own, and he wants to hear the verbal testimony of witnesses under oath. None of the pretrial filings with the court are under oath.

Even the trial memorandums are not submitted under oath. Therefore, they have no probative or evidentiary weight of their own. They are provided simply for the convenience of the judge as a procedural outline of the trial.

There is a standard format which each party must use when preparing its trial memorandum. The format is annexed to the Standing Pretrial Order, and is presented (slightly edited) in Figure 6.1. A significant requirement of the format is that, when complete, it is to be returned directly to the assigned trial judge in Washington, D.C. The judge will retain each memorandum in his personal file of each case that he is calendared to hear. Usually, the judge brings the two memorandums with him, when he enters the courtroom and steps onto the judicial podium.

UNITED STATES TAX COURT

....)
Petitioner(s)) DOCKET NO. _____
v.) Trial Calendar
Commissioner of Internal Revenue,) _____
Respondent) *(city)*
_____) _____
) *(date)*

TRIAL MEMORANDUM FOR PETITIONER / RESPONDENT

1 . ATTORNEYS
  Petitioner: _____ Respondent: _____
  Phone No.: _____ Phone No.: _____

2 . AMOUNTS IN DISPUTE
  <u>Year(s)</u> <u>Deficiencies</u> <u>Additions</u>
  From "90-day letter(s)" by IRS

3 . STIPULATIONS OF FACT
  Issue I ....
  Issue II ....
  Issue III ....

4 . WITNESSES TO BE CALLED

  Name(s) and brief(s) of expected testimony

5 . ESTIMATED TRIAL TIME

6 . SUMMARY OF FACTS

  In chronological narrative form

7 . SYNOPSIS OF LEGAL AUTHORITIES
  Citations of prior court cases involving comparable
  disputive issues

8 . EVIDENTIARY PROBLEMS
  Matters of inadmissible evidence and use of prior
  testimony for impeachment purposes

....

Dated: _____ _____
/s/
Petitioner / Respondent

....

RETURN TO: Judge _____
U.S.Tax Court , Washington, D.C.
Room No.: _____ ; Phone No.: _____

Fig. 6.1 - Format of Trial Memorandum to TC Judge

Entry of Stipulations

Tax Court procedures rely heavily on the parties stipulating to as much of the noncontroversial matters as possible. The idea is to save trial (testimony) time without wrangling over items which are not focal issues. Once a stipulated item is *entered* (meaning: entered in the trial record by the court clerk), it becomes irrefutable evidence thereafter. Because of this irrefutability, TC judges address stipulatory matters as their first order of trial business.

After the petitioner or his attorney and the IRS attorney state their full names for "appearance" (on record) purposes, the judge may ask both parties simultaneously:

Are there any stipulations to be received?

Most often, the IRS attorney answers first: "Yes, Your Honor."

This first-out-of-the-gate response is because the IRS has most to gain by the irrefutability of stipulations. Also, the IRS probably has slipped something over on the petitioner or his attorney. "Slipping something over" is precisely why the IRS exchanges its documents and papers with the petitioner's attorney in that critical 10 seconds as the judge seats himself at the podium.

In general, there are three categories of stipulations, namely:

(1) stipulations of facts
— proposed or agreed
(2) stipulations of recomputation
— proposed or agreed
(3) stipulations of exhibits
— proposed or agreed

The idea is that either party presents its proposed stipulations whether the other party agrees or not. If the parties do indeed agree, they (together) sign as "joint" stipulants. Each stipulation should be numbered: 1, 2, 3, etc. when proposed by the petitioner; A, B, C, etc. when proposed by the IRS, and 1-A, 2-B, 3-C, etc. when agreed to jointly.

Stipulations of fact are presented to the court in the trial memorandum, with a notation that the other party agrees or disagrees with each item stated. Generally, these are facts which are more or less self-evident from those entries on the tax returns, as officially filed with the IRS. The facts identify and confirm particular schedules, attachments, and amounts.

Stipulations of recomputations (if any) are presented to the court in a separate document from the trial memorandum. The recomputations involve the correction of obvious errors and relatively minor items which the parties (usually the petitioner) may have conceded, in order not to distract from the key disputed amounts. More often, recomputations are indeed a joint stipulation, which is so submitted to the trial judge as an irrefutable document of its own.

Stipulation of exhibits constitutes the primary bone of contention between the parties. For reasons of obfuscation, the IRS tends to deluge the court with mountains of extraneous documents. Apparently, the IRS believes that its duty is to do so, under its "preponderance of evidence" theory. All of this, of course, confuses and clouds the core issues in dispute. This is done intentionally because, as we'll explain below, under the "presumption of correctness" of the IRS, confused TC judges are more apt to side with the IRS than with the petitioner. At any rate, the safest stipulatory position of the petitioner is joint agreement on the *authenticity* — NOT ADMISSIBILITY — of any and all exhibits proposed by the IRS. We've already discussed this matter in the latter part of Chapter 5. However, there are practical limits to a petitioner's "no-admissibility" stance.

Objections to Exhibits

When a TC trial judge asks for entry of stipulations, he/she is interested primarily in the admissibility of stipulated exhibits as evidence. Admissibility automatically implies authentication. Furthermore, stipulating to a list of exhibits, without written objections to each objectionable exhibit, automatically implies to the judge admissibility of *all exhibits*.

Stipulating to exhibits saves the judge from being required to rule on the admissibility of each and every document as it is presented during the trial. Every time a judge makes a ruling on the relevancy of evidence, he/she runs the risk of making a "judicial error." Judicial errors form the basis for appeals from Tax Court decisions. Consequently, judges look with disfavor upon too many objections by the petitioner to the volumes of proposed exhibits by the IRS. This puts an air of onus on the petitioner and his counsel.

Being aware of this onus is why the IRS attorney immediately sounds off and says—

Yes, Your Honor. I have the exhibits in a box.

He then hands the clerk a 9" x 12" x 18"-high box of marked documents. The clerk, in turn, places the box on the judge's podium.
The following discourse ensues:

THE COURT: Now, the exhibits are what?
THE IRS: The exhibits are numbered from 1-A to 120-DP.
THE COURT: All right. Are they described in the stipulation or in a separate document?
THE IRS: They are described in the stipulation as to the exhibits.
THE COURT: All right. The stipulation as to the exhibits, together with Exhibits 1-A through 120-DP, is received.
THE IRS: Thank you, Your Honor.

PETITIONER (his attorney): Well, Your Honor, I'd like to make an objection. I hope I'm not going to make the Court angry at me, . . . but I and opposing counsel [the IRS] have a different view as to whether or not that box of documents is all admissible as evidence. The complete set was not given to me until a few moments ago. I haven't had time to examine them carefully.
THE COURT: Oh! They're already in, I take it?
PETITIONER: There are some issues as to relevance, before submitting and putting them into evidence. We've got a tremendous number of documents comprising over 2,000 pages. We'll work it all out eventually, as the witnesses are called. But I'm not going to stipulate that all those 120 documents are relevant.
THE COURT: Okay.

Opening Statements

After the stipulatory matters are out of the way, and objections received, the trial judge may then say—

Now, I've had the opportunity to read both of your trial memorandums. If you want to add anything to that as an opening statement, Mr. _____ [petitioner's attorney], *you go right ahead.*

An *opening statement* is an opportunity for the petitioner or his attorney to restate the core issues in dispute, and to outline the testimony of witnesses and type of evidence that will be presented. It is also opportunity to explain any substitution of witnesses or evidence, or the necessity (if any) for calling a witness out of sequential order. The petitioner may also request that the court exclude all IRS witnesses (if any), until the IRS presents its side of the case.

For opening statements, the court first addresses the petitioner. This is because the petitioner is always the *moving party* in a TC trial. Only the petitioner can bring a case into Tax Court. The IRS cannot do so on its own. It does not have to. The IRS can always assert a tax deficiency (and penalty) regardless of whether it is correct or incorrect. If a taxpayer objects, and he does not file a petition in Tax Court, the IRS simply collects the tax through levy or seizure. Consequently, it is the petitioner to whom the court looks to "move the trial along."

The court also offers the IRS the opportunity to make an opening statement. In most cases, the IRS declines. It does so because it knows that — except only for its allegations of fraud — the entire burden of proof is on the petitioner. As to its fraud burden, the IRS generally refrains from revealing its strategy and evidence at the outset. It wants to keep the petitioner off-guard, and it wants to first hear the petitioner's testimony which it intends to use for impeachment purposes.

"Presumption of Correctness" Theory

Probably the greatest fault and inequity in our entire federal tax system is the PRESUMPTION that the IRS's determination of tax is correct. We know that this is not always so. This is the very reason why Tax Court proceedings were established. Nevertheless, the tax system presumes that the IRS is correct . . . unless expressly contested.

Were this not the case, the IRS would be in a position of having to explain itself on each and every one of the more than 130,000,000 (130 million) or so tax returns filed every year. No matter how much you might detest the IRS, and feel that it — like every other accuser — must prove itself, you have to admit that such would be an administrative impossibility. Massive amounts of revenue into the U.S. Treasury would be seriously curtailed. And government would have to cease operating. While this is a fantasy we all would enjoy, it is unrealistic. Consequently, the Congress, the President, and the courts have come up with the *presumed correct* theory to protect the revenue of government.

The presumed correct theory has been **judicially upheld** in the following situations:

1 — The deficiency was determined on the basis of a wrong theory or unsound or badly expressed reasons. [*Bernstein Estate v. IRS*, 267 F2d 879.]

2 — The IRS raised an alternative theory at the time of trial in which the petitioner did not offer counter-proof. [*Wyandotte Corp. v. IRS*, 352 F2d 530.]

3 — The IRS's determination was based on inadmissible hearsay evidence (a revenue agent's testimony). [*Weimerskirch*, (1977) 69 TC 672.]

4 — The IRS failed (when contested) to provide an explanation of how it arrived at the valuation of the item giving rise to the deficiency. [*Barnes v. IRS*, (1969, CA7) 408 F2d 65.]

5 — Fire had destroyed the books and records prepared by taxpayer's husband; he died prior to trial. [*Sharwell*, TC Memo 1968-89.]

6 — The deficiency was based on the arbitrary disallowance of costs of good sold because the examining agent was denied access to the books and records. [*Durovic*, (1970) 54 TC 1364.]

These and other judicial rulings on the presumption of correctness of the IRS have sent the wrong message to that agency. The message is that the IRS can be arbitrary to any degree that it wants, and it can knowingly assert an incorrect tax or penalty and still be presumed correct. This policy fosters arrogance and abusiveness by the IRS.

Armed with its "presumed correct" theory, the IRS can maintain its intransigent stance fight up into Tax Court. It never has to explain or correct itself. Thus, the Tax Court *starts off with* the presumption theory. This automatically puts all burden of proving incorrectness on the petitioner.

We want to emphasize that the Tax Court's startoff position is a **presumption** of correctness only. It is NOT PROOF of correctness. Otherwise, there would be nothing for the Tax Court to do. Its job is to *redetermine* the amount of tax and penalty asserted by the IRS. Therefore, in order for the Tax Court to do its job, the petitioner must first overcome the presumption theory.

Overcoming the Presumption

The presumption of correctness is a separate and distinct legal concept from that of the petitioner's burden of proof. The presumption has to be overcome and destroyed first. Then the petitioner has to follow through with proving the incorrectness of the IRS, or at least that some other amount is more correct.

Overcoming the presumption destroys it as a fallback (do nothing, say nothing) position for the IRS. The PRESUMPTION IS NOT EVIDENCE. It is simply a tactical starting point for convenience of the court.

To overcome the initial correctness presumption, the petitioner must introduce **competent and relevant** evidence. [*Griffin v. IRS*, 285 F2d 91; *Niederkrome v. IRS*, 266 F2d 238; *A & A Tool Co. v. IRS*, 182 F2d 300.] If the petitioner fails to introduce such evidence, the presumption continues. [*O'Dwyer* (1957) 28 TC 698(A), aff'd 266 F2d 575, cert den 361 US 862.] In other words, where the only evidence presented by the petitioner consists of uncorroborated, self-serving statements of denial, the presumption stands.

What is competent and relevant evidence?

Answer: It is that which, when properly presented to the Court, could — with sufficient deductive reasoning — *support a contrary result* from that which has been asserted by the IRS. The evidence must support a good-faith position that, perhaps indeed, the IRS could be wrong. It is that constructive showing of wrongness that takes the wind out of the IRS's sails.

For example, suppose certain expenditures were made and were claimed as a business expense on the petitioner's tax return. The IRS disallowed the entire amount without, as it does so often, giving any reason or convincing explanation. Tentatively, the IRS is presumed correct. But if the amount and purpose of the expenditures can be corroborated with "third-party" evidence, and it can be shown that the petitioner reasonably relied on an applicable section of the IR Code where the expenditure might indeed be allowed, the presumption is destroyed. All that needs to be shown is that another finding could apply.

Once the presumption is destroyed, it disappears as to that particular issue to which the evidence is directed. It is not destroyed with respect to other disputive issues for which competent evidence has yet to be introduced. The overcomed issue then has to be decided on the basis of *all evidence* before the Court . . . without further consideration of the presumption.

So important is the presumption theory, and the necessity for overcoming it, that we present a summary depiction of the situation in Figure 6.2. As a petitioner in Tax Court, Figure 6.2 is intended to impress upon you one unrelenting realization. You must destroy the presumption separately for each and every issue in dispute. This is your cold, hard *first hurdle* of participation in a Tax Court trial.

Burden of Proof (Rule 142)

In the vast majority of Tax Court issues, the burden of proof is smack-dab on the petitioner. Only on issues of fraud and other exceptional assertions is the burden ever upon the IRS. As repugnant to our sense of justice as this may be, said burden has been held not to be an unconstitutional denial of due process. [*Rockwell v. IRS* (1975, CA 9) 512 F2d 882, cert den 423 US 1015.] Thus, shouldering all burden of proof is the second evidentiary hurdle that a petitioner must endure in Tax Court.

The TC rule on point is Rule 142: Burden of Proof. Subrule 142(a), General, says—

*The burden of proof **shall be upon the petitioner**, except as otherwise provided by statute or determined by the Court; and except that, in respect of any new matter, increases in deficiency, and affirmative defenses, pleaded in the Answer [to the Petition], it shall be upon the respondent [IRS]. [Emphasis added.]*

As to the IRS's allegations of fraud, subrule 142(b) says—

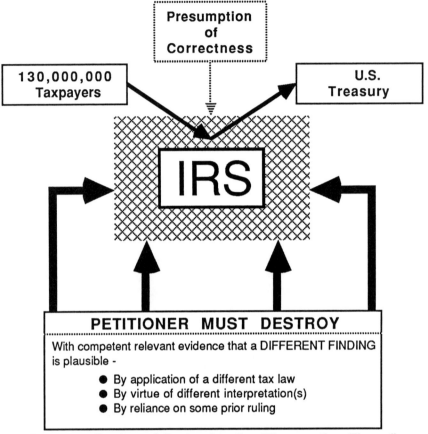

Fig. 6.2 - Burden of Destroying the "Presumption Theory"

*In any case involving the issue of fraud with intent to evade tax, the burden of proof **in respect of that issue** [only] is on the respondent [IRS], and that burden of proof is to be carried **by clear and convincing evidence**. [Emphasis added.]*

The general burden rule is that the petitioner must submit sufficient evidence to convince the court that the IRS has indeed erred. The degree of error must be of substance and not just some de minimis amount. The court must conclude on its own that: "Yes, the IRS has incorrectly determined the amount of tax and/or penalty." When this point is reached, the petitioner has met his *initial* burden of proof.

There is a problem when meeting one's burden of proof against the IRS. You are dealing with a "moving target." The moment you show competently that the IRS has erred, the IRS comes up with an alternate stance — be it reasonable, wild, or ludicrous — to maintain that its determination was correct. It engages in a shifting strategy of proposing to the court one alternative stance after another.

Every time the IRS proposes an alternative stance, the petitioner has to refocus his testimony and evidence to again overcome the presumption of correctness of the alternative stance. He also has to follow through with carrying his burden (against the alternative stance) that — again — the IRS has erred.

It is not necessary that the petitioner prove the amount of error: just that an error of substance does exist. Once this threshold is reached, it becomes the duty of the Tax Court to determine the amount of error by redetermining the correct tax. If the petitioner is able to show that he owes some amount smaller than that asserted by the IRS, or that he owes no additional tax at all, so much the better.

Examination of Witnesses

The real virtue of a Tax Court trial is the opportunity for the petitioner (and/or his spouse) to testify in his own behalf. It is also an opportunity for the petitioner to call upon other persons, knowledgeable of relevant facts, to testify in his behalf. When properly introduced, and sworn, the court must hear their testimony. The court cannot ignore the personal statements of facts and circumstances, the way the IRS does in its everyday treatment of taxpayers.

Theoretically, the petitioner has the right to call upon various IRS agents and officials as "hostile" witnesses. Doing so is an exercise in futility. The IRS bureaucracy shields and coaches its employees to reveal nothing of constructive benefit to the petitioner. The IRS will even go so far as to send a key IRS witness on unscheduled leave, to avoid having such person appear at trial. (See page 9-22.) The reality is that even if, through subpoenas, you can force an IRS employee to attend, you cannot impeach him (or her). You have no access to prior documentation or testimony of such person executed under oath or under penalty of perjury.

There is a set sequence of procedures when examining any person called to the witness stand in Tax Court. It is a four-step sequence, namely: direct, redirect, cross, and recross. Two steps are by the petitioner — direct and redirect; two steps are by the IRS

— cross and recross. The sequence is reversed, of course, when the IRS calls its own witnesses. We present this four-step examination process schematically in Figure 6.3.

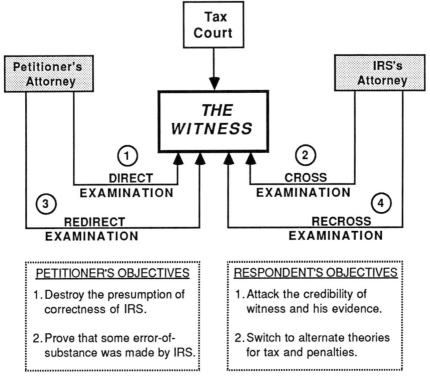

Fig. 6.3 - The Examination Process of a TC Trial Witness

The idea behind the Figure 6.3 examination sequence is to enable the court to come to its own conclusion about the credibility of each witness. The court wants to decide for itself whether all, part, or none of the testimony of each witness is believable.

The degree of believability of a witness rests upon the adversarial nature of the judicial system. One adversary — the IRS — has opportunity to rebut, and re-rebut, the testimony of the petitioner's witnesses. The petitioner, in turn, has opportunity to rebut, and re-rebut, the testimony of the IRS's witnesses. Rebuttal and cross-rebuttal is the means — allegedly — for flushing out the facts of truth in a witness's testimony.

What really happens is that the IRS often raises a lot of "red herrings." It does so, intentionally, to confuse the court and create doubt in its mind. When the IRS has been proven to have erred, it can become a vicious and vindictive adversary.

Books, Records, & Papers

More than in any other tribunal, the Tax Court relies heavily on documentary evidence. It needs this evidence to properly determine the applicable tax law and to properly determine the correct tax. It needs to see for itself those books, records, papers, receipts, invoices, letters, statements, cancelled checks, and other documents that the petitioner used, or should have used, when preparing his tax return(s) for the year(s) in dispute.

For Tax Court purposes, relevant documents and things "speak for themselves." The court becomes fixated on this uncorroborated maxim. This is why TC judges are eager for the opposing parties to stipulate to the admissibility of as much documentary evidence as possible. As a result, the trial judge tends to ignore the testimony of witnesses regarding the relevancy and materiality of the documents received. Its fixation on documents is a disturbing weakness of the Tax Court. This weakness explains why the IRS tries to inundate the court with voluminous exhibits, whether truly relevant and material or not. TC judges are like other human beings; they tend to skim-read only the highlights of the documents in their possession. They can be misled by such skim-reading.

Consequently, the petitioner (and/or his counsel) must not let the IRS introduce a "pile of documents" en masse. The petitioner must challenge each and every document as to its relevancy (to the issue in dispute) **and** as to its materiality (to the error by the IRS). This challenge applies whether the documents are government-agency prepared, third-party prepared, extractionally prepared (from multiple-page books and records), or IRS prepared. Documents prepared by the petitioner (and/or his spouse) should be offered as evidence, only after establishing their relevancy and materiality, and after allowing the IRS to also challenge.

The only evidentiary area where the petitioner should show challenge restraint is authentication of the electronic reproduction of documents. On this point, TC Rule 143(d)(1), Documentary Evidence: Copies, says—

> *A **clearly legible** copy of any book, record, paper, or document may be offered directly in evidence in lieu of the original, where there is no objection, or where the original is available but admission of a copy is authorized by the Court. . . Where the original is admitted in evidence, a clearly legible copy may be substituted later for the original or **such part thereof as may be material or relevant**.* [Emphasis added.]

Subrule 143(d)(1) is intended only to simplify the otherwise tedious and time-consuming authentication procedures at trial. Nothing in the entire Rule 143: Evidence, requires the petitioner to succumb to the stipulatory barrage of photocopied documents prepared and offered by the IRS. The petitioner has the right to examine in a timely manner all such documents. Said examination automatically implies authentication, if no objections are raised. As we stressed before in Chapter 5, authentication DOES NOT automatically imply admissibility of said documentation as evidence at trial.

Notice of Demonstrative Evidence

TC judges are human. They, too, can get confused over the probative value of each piece of paper in the barrage of documentation before them. Things might be different if the court were not so fixated on the maxim that "documents speak for themselves." This is not always so. Individual documents need explanation, and mass groupings of documents need sorting and sequencing into a sensible roadmap. This is the role that *demonstrative evidence* plays.

Demonstrative evidence is a diagrammatic presentation of pertinent facts and circumstances as viewed by the presenter. Obviously, such "evidence" is biased and self-serving. Therefore, it is not admissible as competent evidence in the cold factual sense. It is admissible **only as an aid** to the party presenting it. Rarely does the IRS ever need to present demonstrative evidence. It can always rely on its safe-harbor presumption of correctness and on the burden of proof being on the petitioner.

To be most effective, demonstrative evidence is prepared in large poster form (2 ft x 3 ft or so) for convenient display and viewing by all who are present in the court. Preferably, there should be only **one** such display. Select one poster (among several alternatives) that best summarizes the trail of evidence that is likely to most impress the trial judge.

To be admissible as an aid, the petitioner must notice and serve upon the IRS photocopies of the intended display(s), at least 30 days before trial. This gives the IRS time to prepare its objection in court and to cross-examine the demonstrative presenter.

A typical said notice to the IRS might read as follows:

NOTICE OF INTENTION TO USE DEMONSTRATIVE EVIDENCE

The petitioner hereby puts the respondent [IRS] on notice that he intends to use the attached exhibits for demonstration purposes only, to aid the petitioner's testimony in explaining the nature of his Issue II expenditures.

Dated:_____   _____*/s/*_____
                                             Attorney for Petitioners

Once the demonstrative presentation is over, it is a good idea to **leave it on display**, while the trial continues. Let the judge, the IRS, and the witnesses subconsciously glance at it from time to time. If you do this, make sure that its focal message is succinct, clear, and informative. Although its probative value is minimal or none at all, its lasting-impression value is what you want. All you can hope to do is dilute — and perhaps divert — the court's obsession with the barrage of evidentiary documents that the IRS will interpose.

Rule 150: Record of Proceedings

Except for small tax cases (disputes of $10,000 or less per year), all Tax Court trials are stenographically recorded. From the recordings, a typewritten transcript — indexed and paginated — is prepared. The trial transcript is retained by the Chief Clerk as a permanent record of each docketed hearing.

The trial transcript becomes an important evidentiary document in the event of appeal or subsequent litigation by the same taxpayer/petitioner. Even though no subsequent litigation may be contemplated, the transcript becomes an important document for extracting factual statements, misstatements, and allegations by IRS agents and officials, and other government-agency witnesses who may have testified at trial. The trial transcript is the ONLY OPPORTUNITY that a taxpayer/petitioner ever has of *capturing* the IRS under oath! This, alone, is worth all the effort and expense of the ordeal.

On this point, TC Rule 150(a) reads in full as follows:

*Hearings and trials before the Court **shall** be stenographically reported or otherwise recorded, and **a transcript thereof shall be made** if, in the opinion of the Court or Judge presiding at a hearing or trial, a **permanent record** is deemed appropriate. Transcripts shall be supplied to the parties and other persons at such charges as may be fixed or approved by the Court.* [Emphasis added.]

The term "hearings" refers to various pre-trial and post-trial motions pertaining to points of law and points of procedure. It is not often that these matters are transcribed. Memorandums prepared by the opposing counsel suffice for ordinary record purposes.

In other words, either party — or *any person* — may pay the stenographic charge and obtain, and retain, an official transcript of any Tax Court trial in which he has an interest. The excerpts that we quote to you in Chapters 7, 8, 9, and 10 are taken directly from such official transcripts. These transcripts are permanently retained by the Tax Court.

In the case of exhibits received by the court, no permanent record is made of them. Upon written application to the Chief Clerk of the Tax Court, either party may request that all or a portion of the documents be returned. Otherwise, after 90 days after the TC decision becomes final, the exhibits will be destroyed. [TC Rule 143(d)(2).] This is why the use of authentic photocopies of the originals of the proposed exhibits is encouraged.

Trial Court Setting Summarized

In the next four chapters, we are going to take you into a real life Tax Court trial room. We want to expose you to the activities there. We want you to sense, feel, and read the adversarial "gutter fighting" that goes on between the petitioner and the IRS.

To help you visualize the Tax Court setting at time of trial, we present Figure 6.4. The courtroom is located in a designated federal building, usually on a floor near regional IRS offices. Each courtroom is surrounded by solid walls (no windows) with only one

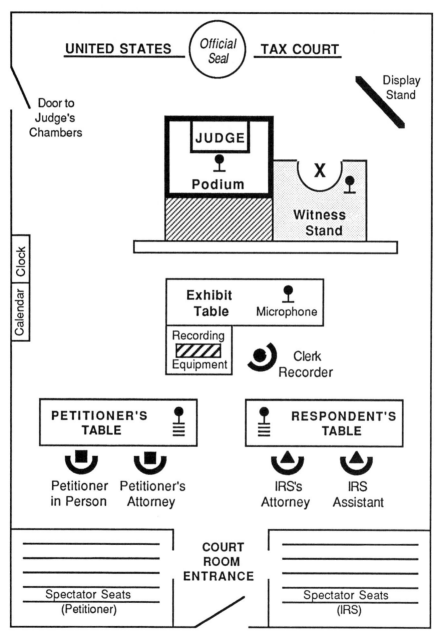

Fig. 6.4 - Arrangements of Participants in a Tax Court Trialroom

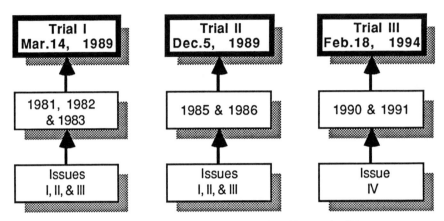

Fig. 6.5 - Tax Court Trials and Tax Years in Dispute

general entrance to it. There is a separate entrance that the trial judge uses when he leaves his adjacent office chambers to enter the courtroom. Picture yourself as that judge.

As the judge, you should note that the petitioner's table is to your right; the respondent's table — the IRS — is to your left. In some TC courtrooms, movable nameplates are used to designate which table is which. There is also an exhibit table, to and from which the clerk recorder places and retrieves documents and exhibits used by the judge, the witness, the petitioner, and the IRS.

Note also in Figure 6.4 that there are five speaker locations. These are indicated by small microphone symbols. During the time the judge is seated at his podium, no persons in the courtroom are allowed to speak, other than parties to the trial.

Tax Court proceedings rarely attract the attention of the news media, TV crews, or book authors. The technical aspects of tax disputes simply do not evoke the pizzazz and appeal of "Who-done-it" thrillers. Consequently, you'll not find TC transcripts and testimony in bookstores and libraries. This is why we've gone out of our way to present the author's first-hand experience with the true ordeal of the verbal exchanges that take place at Tax Court trials.

For summary and focus purposes for upcoming Chapters 7, 8, 9, and 10, we present Figure 6.5. This figure gives a foretaste of the span of time involved when going into Tax Court for a particular tax return year.

7

AT TRIAL: ISSUE I

Issue I Addresses Sec. 170(c)(1) Of The IR Code Re The Deductibility Of An Alleged Charitable Contribution To The Social Security Administration. At Age 62 And FULLY INSURED Under Social Security, Petitioner Computed His Actuarial Lifetime Benefits At $88,583. Instead Of Applying For Said Benefits, He Renounced Them Irrevocably In Favor Of Those "Older Americans" In Greater Need. The IRS Argues That There Was No Gift Because The Word "Gift" Was Not Used In The Renunciation Letter, And Because No Check For $88,583 Was Written. Fortunately, The Social Security System Was SAVED In 1984.

In this and the next three chapters, position yourself as the trial judge. You are sitting at the courtroom podium facing the petitioner and his attorney, and the IRS's attorney and his assistant. The trial memoranda are in, stipulations (and their objections) have been received, procedural matters have been discussed, and you've heard a short opening statement by the petitioner's attorney.

Before you is Issue I. As you understand it, the petitioner alleges to have made an unconditional public gift of his lifetime Social Security benefits to the Social Security Administration. For this alleged gift, petitioner claimed a charitable deduction on Schedule A of his Form 1040 tax return, using the actuarial dollar value as the amount of the gift. The IRS's "determination" is that no gift was made, and, consequently, there is no deduction to be allowed.

You are satisfied from the information in the petitioner's trial memorandum that the presumption of correctness of the IRS has been overcome. The memorandum cited the existing tax law on charitable deductions and a little-known public law on money gifts to the Social Security Administration.

The petitioner's attorney has made it clear that, as to Issue I, there'll be only one witness: the petitioner (husband) himself. Although the petitioner filed a joint return with his wife, it is the petitioner alone who made the alleged gift. His statements under oath will be signified as: WITNESS (P). The (P) is for "petitioner."

The IRS's attorney indicated that he, too, would present one witness, addressing Issue I. Said witness was identified as a representative of the Social Security Administration. His statements under oath will be signified as: WITNESS (R). The (R) is for "respondent."

Editorial "Culling" Necessary

The same petitioner is involved in Issues I, II, III, and IV, which we intend to present in separate chapters. In trial transcript form, all issues are confusingly intertwined. The entire official transcript on these issues consists of 530 pages. This number is more than twice the length of this book. Naturally, we have to do some culling and editing.

We promise to be objective about our culling. We will try not to slant the factual matters for or against either party. Since we already know the outcome of each of the four key issues (I, II, III, and IV), we can eliminate those statements which had no influence on each TC judge's final decision.

In any court proceeding, the practice is to have each witness step forward, raise his hand for oath, state his name, spell it out, and recite a short biographical sketch of his educational background and work experience. We will dispense with most of this.

Questions, objections, and statements by the petitioner's attorney will be signified as: PETITIONER. Questions, objections, and statements by the IRS's attorney will be signified as: THE IRS. Neither the petitioner's attorney nor the IRS's attorney are testifying under oath (standard procedure). Consequently, their statements do not constitute admissible evidence. Other than for transitional continuity, we'll omit most of such statements.

Also for transitional continuity, we organize the testimony of each witness into discrete subparts. Legal strategists like to skip around, mix things up, argue over exhibits, so as to confuse the issues. We'll try to group things logically, the way the real judge does when forming his own decision.

All four key issues (I, II, III, and IV) span tax years 1981 through 1991. As to Issue I (public gift), we'll focus on tax year 1981 only. This is the "gift year"; all subsequent years are "carryover" years. If no gift was made, the carryover years are irrelevant. If a gift was made, the carryover years are purely mathematical computations based on the money value of the 1981 gift. Thus, judicially, for Issue I purposes, the focus need only be on 1981.

Leadoff Testimony: Letter to President

After Witness (P) gave a short description of his background, petitioner's attorney addressed the court saying—

PETITIONER: Your Honor, I would like to elicit some testimony about the charitable contribution on petitioner's Schedule A, Itemized Deductions, of his 1981 return. I'd like to start with Exhibit 22-V.
THE COURT: All right.
PETITIONER: Mr._____, do you have Exhibit 22-V?
WITNESS (P):   Yes, I do.

> *Editorial Note*: As long as the same attorney and same witness are speaking, we indicate questions with the letter "Q" and answers with the letter "A." This makes for smoother reading.

Q: Could you refer to that, please?
A: 22-V. I have it. Okay.
Q: Now, this is a letter that you sent to President Reagan on May 12th, 1981?
A: That's correct. That's the date.
Q: What was the purpose of sending this letter?
A: Well, it was to indicate that I agreed with the President on his comments to a joint session of Congress on April 28th concerning the Social Security system and its pending fiscal bankruptcy.

The following day, he came out with a proclamation designating May, 1981 as "Older Americans Month." He invited voluntary efforts from young and old alike to help senior citizens, those in greater need.

The next day, the President was interviewed on national TV, asking what he meant by his proclamation. He responded that, well, those senior citizens who could afford to do so might consider -- it was only a thought -- might consider giving up their Social Security benefits for those in greater need.

So, therefore, my letter was to respond to the climate at that time. The Social Security was in dire fiscal crisis: $160 billion actuarially underfunded. So, in responding to that climate, I renounced irrevocably forever all of my Social Security benefits.

Q: I notice that you notarized your letter to the President?

A: I went to the effort to have it notarized because I wanted it to be recorded in the official records of the Social Security Administration.

PETITIONER: Your Honor, I would like the witness to look at and direct your attention to Exhibit 24-X.

THE COURT: Okay. 24-X.

Q: Mr._____, is this a letter that you received from the Commissioner of Social Security?

A: Yes, I did.

Q: Does this acknowledge their receipt of your letter to President Reagan?

A: Yes, it does.

PETITIONER: Your Honor, I'd like to direct you at this point to Exhibit 23-W.

THE COURT: All right.

Q: Mr._____, did you send this letter (Exhibit 23-W) to the Secretary of Health and Human Services?

A: Yes, I did.

Q: And what was your purpose in sending this letter?

A: Well, I also saw him on television. He was pointing out the actuarial deficit of the Social Security system. He seemed to be trying to solicit ideas and suggestions as to how the system could be strengthened, and since this was exactly ten days after I'd sent my letter to President Reagan, I thought I would write him and tell him that I had made one effort to strengthen the system. I pointed out the savings there could be to the national budget if other seniors were encouraged to do likewise [renounce their benefits]. I urged him to consider this idea and propose it to other members of Congress and to various committees involving Social Security.

Reliance on Public Law 92-603

Petitioner's attorney continued his direct examination of the petitioner as witness, as follows—

Q: We are going to switch gears now. Could you look at your 1981 Return? It is Exhibit 5-E.
A: Yes, I have it.
Q: Can you look at the portion that refers to charitable deductions?
A: Yes, that's on Schedule A; yes, I have it.
Q: What, if any, deduction did you take for your renunciation of your Social Security benefits?
A: I took approximately a $15,000 deduction and I annotated that with Code Section 170(c)(1), Social Security entitlement (62) [meaning: age 62]. I also pointed out that I was limited by the carryover rules.
Q: Prior to preparing your return, what research, if any, did you do to determine if there was a legal basis for that deduction?
A: When President Reagan first mentioned this idea approximately April 29th of 1981, I called my Congressman's office. I told his administrative assistant, "The President has made some suggestions about trying to strengthen the Social Security system, and I'd like to give all my benefits to it." I was told that there was a new law that would permit this and that they were going to call the Social Security Administration.

They called me back and said, "Yes, there's a new law but perhaps you ought to follow up more on your own." At this point, I went down to the law library and looked through the Social Security Act. I ran across Section 401(i), which is labeled "Gifts and Bequests to Social Security." That seemed to fit the bill that it could be done.

I then looked beyond that to see what the enabling legislation was, the public law behind it, and then uncovered Public Law 92-603, Section 132(g). This was quite a bit more explicit in terms of being a charitable contribution and also being for exclusively public purposes.

> *Editorial Note*: Public Law 92-603, Section 132: Acceptance of Money Gifts Made Unconditionally to Social Security, was enacted October 30, **1972**. The IRS, to this date, has never implemented this law with specifically applicable regulations. Its nearest approach is Revenue Ruling 82-169 of October **1982** which acknowledges "voluntary contributions" to Social Security.

Unfortunately, I couldn't find any regulations in the Internal Revenue Code that would somehow tie into this part of Public Law 92-603. The nearest I could find was Regulation 1.170(a)-6(a). It said that a contribution deduction would be allowed if a donor with an income interest in a trust [such as the Social Security Tust Fund] would give up his entire interest in such trust income.

There was no explanation as to how this could be done. So I used the disclaimer procedures of Section 2518 which says that "you shall not receive the benefits but shall disclaim them at the appropriate time when you first become eligible to collect them." So it was on this basis that I undertook the renunciation [of my lifetime Social Security benefits].

Valuation Aspects

Further continuing with his direct examination of the petitioner as witness, petitioner's attorney asked—

Q: What, if any, background or research did you do regarding the valuation of your renunciated benefits?
A: To establish the valuation, first of all I'd written this letter to Commissioner Svahn [of Social Security] in June or July of 1981 asking him specifically for my actuarial value. I didn't get any response until October 5th of 1981, in which a figure of $60,000 was mentioned as the likely actuarial present value. But he indicated that many of my prior earnings records were incomplete, so I found it necessary to write back through my Congressman's office again to the Social Security Administration.

At that point in time, it was getting near tax filing time and I thought, "Well, look, I can't wait for another answer from Social Security in Washington, D.C." So I went down in person to the local Social Security office. They gave me an official form which estimated my Social Security benefits at $439 per month commencing May, 1981. They wouldn't give me their life-expectancy tables. So, I had to go again through my Congressman.

I got the life-expectancy tables quite hurriedly because they were photocopied by the local office [of Social Security] and sent to me by my Congressman.

When I got the life-expectancy tables -- 16.8 years in my case -- I applied the monthly benefits to my life expectancy and came up with the figure of $88,583. This is what I entered on my return as a charitable contribution for 1981.

PETITIONER: That's good enough for that part. That's all the testimony I have at this time, Your Honor.

Cross Examination Re Exhibit 22-V

Now starts the cross-examination on Issue I by the IRS. It is "standard procedure" that the IRS be allowed to direct its questioning in as caustic and penetrating a manner as it sees fit. Its objective — properly so — is to discredit the testimony of any taxpayer/petitioner on the witness stand. The idea is to break through the witness's defense shield to establish contrary facts. Reference to Exhibit 22-V is the renunciatory letter which the petitioner (witness) wrote to the President on May 12, 1981.

At this point, the trial judge addresses the IRS's attorney—

THE COURT: You may cross-examine.
THE IRS: Thank you, Your Honor. Mr. _____, a b o u t your claimed renunciation of your Social Security benefits. Could you refer to Joint Exhibit 22-V?
WITNESS (P): Yes.
Q: At the time you wrote this letter, did you believe that the Social Security system was actuarially bankrupt?
A: Yes, I did.
Q: Did you believe it was mandatory enslavement?
A: Yes, and I'll explain if you want.
Q: Did you believe it was morally fraudulent upon the future generations of this nation?
A: Yes, I did.
Q: Okay. And you're not a tax protester?

PETITIONER: I'm going to object. I don't know whether he's a tax protester or not, but that's certainly not an issue.
THE COURT: Well, that calls for an opinion so I won't require him [the witness] to answer unless he wants to.

THE IRS: Are you a tax protester, Mr. _____?
THE COURT: [to the witness] I will not require you to answer if you have any reservations about what he means by "tax protester."
WITNESS (P): I decline to answer it.
THE COURT: All right. Go ahead, counsel.
Q: This letter, Joint Exhibit 22-V, represents your renunciation in gifting of benefits?
A: Yes. [See Figure 7.1.]
Q: Can you show me where the words "gift" or "donate" appear in that letter?
A: [reading from the letter] "This renunciation," paragraph three, "is undertaken as a specific example of how the Social Security can be strengthened for those who want it and need it."
Q: But does it say "gift" or "donate" anywhere in the letter?
A: I think that was implied.
THE COURT: No, but does it say it?
WITNESS (P): Does not say it; that's correct.

Continuing Cross: Money Matters

The IRS attorney continued his cross-examination of the petitioner as witness, as follows—

Q: You also say that this claimed gift was for exclusively public purposes?
A: That's correct.
Q: Does it say "exclusively for a public purpose" somewhere in this document, Joint Exhibit 22-V?
A: It doesn't use that phrase, no.
Q: Also in the same letter, second page, paragraph six, you requested that the President help in establishing administrative procedures for accomplishing certain tax credits?
A: Yes, that's paragraph six.
Q: Did the President give you this idea of claiming a tax credit for Social Security benefits?
A: No, the President's idea was, for those who could afford it, to give up their Social Security benefits.

Q: Do you have a cancelled check that substantiates your claimed cash contribution of $88,583 on your 1981 return, Exhibit 5-E?
PETITIONER: I'm going to object, only that he didn't claim a cash contribution.

May 12, 1981

Dear Mr. President:

Re: RENUNCIATION OF
SOCIAL SECURITY BENEFITS

Whereas on January 31, 1981 I became age 62, covered under the
Social Security system, and eligible to commence receiving benefits
thereunder, but to this date having claimed no benefits whatsoever;

NOW THEREFORE -
I, the undersigned, _____[the petitioner]_____ , do hereby renounce
irrevocably forever all right, title, and claim to any and all Social Security
benefits to which I might otherwise be entitled by virtue of my employment
earnings since 1940, my self-employment earnings since 1970, and any
applicable earnings of my beloved wife.

This renunciation is undertaken as a specific example of how the
Social Security system can be strengthened for those who want it and
need it...

IN WITNESS WHEREOF, -

_____/s/_____
[Petitioner]

Fig. 7.1 - Focal Paragraphs in Exhibit 22-V Re Issue I

THE COURT: Go ahead. Let him answer. Obviously he didn't,
but you can get it in the record.
WITNESS (P): Cash also means -- debt forgiveness or cancellation
of debts.
THE COURT: Well, do you have a check? Just answer.
WITNESS (P): No, I don't have a check on that.
THE IRS: Do you have a receipt of any kind that
acknowledges your contribution of $88,583?
A: No, other than that letter from—
Q: [interrupting the witness before allowing him to complete his
answer] Thank you. Do you have--

PETITIONER: Your Honor, just so I understand the Rules of Evidence here, I think he can answer and then explain his answer.
THE COURT: Well, yes, he can. What do you think might be?
WITNESS (P): I thought the letter from Commissioner Svahn [of Social Security] was the acknowledgment and receipt of my renunciation letter.
THE IRS: But did it say that they acknowledge their receipt specifically of $88,583?
A: No.
Q: Do you have a cancelled check that substantiates your claimed contribution for your 1982 return?
A: No.
Q: Do you have a cancelled check that substantiates your claimed cash contribution for your 1983 return?
A: No, I don't, but you know that these are carryover years and even if I had a check on the first year, there would be no check for the second and third years.
Q: You don't have any receipt that shows specifically that Social Security actually received the exact amount that you have claimed on those returns?
A: No. I have a letter saying that they received my renunciation letter on June 2nd, 1981.

Continuing Cross: Life Expectancy

Further continuing his cross-examination of the petitioner as witness, the IRS attorney asks—

Q: When you valued the gift by the actuarial tables, you claimed that you would live approximately 16.8 years; do you recall?
A: Yes.
Q: It is possible that you wouldn't live that long?
A: I've lived half that length already.
Q: But it is possible that at the time, you wouldn't live that long? You could get into an accident, right?
A: I can't answer that. I'm still alive.
Q: But there is a possibility that you would not?

PETITIONER: I'm going to object based on speculation.
THE COURT: I'll sustain that. Obviously, actuarial tables are an average and some people live way less and some people live way more. I can't imagine why he won't go ahead and answer it, but I

don't think it's something you can require him to answer. He doesn't claim to be an expert on actuarial tables.

THE IRS: Your Honor, I just needed the Court to take judicial notice of the fact that Mr. _____ probably could live longer than 16.8 years. He could also live less.

THE COURT: Anybody can.

THE IRS: Thank you, Your Honor. No further questions.

The Redirect Examination

Redirect examination is opportunity for the moving party on an issue — in this instance, the petitioner's attorney — to try to clear up any dangling or ambiguous testimony that might be on the record. It is also opportunity to rebut any potentially damaging evidence that might have been brought forth by the IRS. Redirect and recross are usually not very long, as both parties have pretty much presented their cases in the direct- and cross-examination processes. The court asks: "Any redirect?"

PETITIONER: Yes, Your Honor.

Q: [addressing the witness] Those deductions that you took for charitable contributions on your '81, '82, and '83 returns: What statute were they based on?

A: They were based on the actual Code Section 170(c)(1); exactly as I identified on the return.

Q: Did you feel that there was an insignificant chance that your returns would be audited?

A: No, I expected they'd be audited. I filed them early. I claimed a rather large deduction. I knew they would be audited.

Q: What happened after the audit(s)?

A: I was told that all my deductions would be disallowed. I asked for explanations and for the IRS agents to show me procedural guidelines as to how otherwise I could make my renunciatory gift. There was a statutory basis for my position. I was getting no response. I was getting threats of penalties. They [the IRS] could never quote a regulation, and they never quoted me any law saying that I could not renounce my Social Security benefits.

Q: Why did you let this matter come to Tax Court?

A: Because I wanted to bring this matter to the attention of a court of competent jurisdiction. I wanted to get the matter resolved.

Q: You wanted to get it over with?

A: Yes. I gave my entire lifetime Social Security benefits to the Government. I didn't want to go on eight years [1981 to 1989] like I've been going on to find an answer for something I think was a generous act to the Government.

PETITIONER: I don't have any further questions, Your Honor.
THE COURT: All right. Anything further?
THE IRS: Nothing further, Your Honor.
THE COURT: We'll take a very short recess. The witness [petitioner] may be excused.

Witness (R): Social Security Official

After recess and after the judge re-entered the courtroom and sat down at the podium, the judge said—

THE COURT: You may call your next witness.
THE IRS: Your Honor, the Respondent would like to call Mr. _____ of the Social Security Administration.
THE COURT: All right. Go ahead. [Witness (R) was duly sworn and took the stand.]
THE IRS: Can you describe for us the purpose of the Social Security system?
THE COURT: Be kind of brief about it.
WITNESS (R): It's a system that's designed to provide replacement income for individuals when they lose their primary source of income because they retire or become disabled or the wage earner dies.
Q: Can you define for us when an individual is considered in an insured status?
A: Insured status means that an individual has worked for the required length of time under the system in order to be eligible to receive benefits. "Fully insured status" means 40 quarters or more.
Q: Can you define for the Court what is meant by entitlement to benefits?
A: Entitlement means that a person meets the insured status requirements, meets the age 62 requirement, and has filed an application.
Q: Is it possible to make gifts to the Social Security Trust Fund?
A: Yes, there's a provision in the law for the trustee of the trust accounts to receive contributions?
Q: Do you know what kind of contributions can be accepted?

A : Well, usually we would receive cash contributions or someone would give us a check as a donation.

Q : Is Mr. _____ [petitioner] entitled to received benefits?

A : The only way he can be entitled is if he has filed an application.

PETITIONER: Your Honor, I'm going to object to this on the grounds that it is speculation by the witness.

THE COURT: Well, I think that it's clear. The Social Security law and regulations and everything else tell you that you can only receive benefits if you filed an application. That's written right in them, isn't it?

WITNESS (R): That's correct.

THE COURT: All right. Now, what do these two documents [110-DF and 120-DP] tell you?

WITNESS (R): They tell me that Mr. _____ has not filed an application because he's not on the record as receiving benefits.

THE IRS: No further questions, Your Honor.

THE COURT: All right. You [petitioner's attorney] may cross-examine.

PETITIONER: No questions, Your Honor.

THE COURT: You [witness (R)] are excused.

Postscript and Review

Altogether, Issue I dragged on from May 1981 to May 1989. This spanned a total of eight years!

The Tax Court is not concerned with how long an issue drags on, nor with what the legal costs might be to the petitioner. Nor is the Tax Court concerned with what benefits the government derives or doesn't derive by the voluntary efforts of well-meaning citizens. The court is only concerned with the applicable tax law and regulations, if any, in effect at the time of the origin of a tax dispute. When a law is unclear or ambiguous, the court is not required to embark on any "creative interpretation" of it.

Within the 8-year Issue I time span, the fiscal crisis (alleged bankruptcy) of the Social Security system had abated. The Social Security Amendments Act of 1983 **increased** the amount of social security and medicare tax, and required, commencing in 1984, that all recipients of social security benefits be "means taxed" on those benefits. This was a landmark change. Prior to 1984, the receipt of social security benefits was never income taxed. In this manner, the

Social Security system was "saved." Whether the TC judge hearing the Issue I testimony was influenced by this political reality in 1989 is not clear.

Nevertheless, following the Issue I testimony, the court stated orally that—

> *Now, I will say just right out; I have no problem with the fact that there was not a gift if, for no other reason, it was not accepted. Every one of those exhibit letters that came back from anybody connected with the Social Security Administration said that they would not accept a lump sum gift. They kept telling the petitioner that: "All we will accept is—you go ahead and apply for your monthly benefits, and then you can either give us your checks back when you get them, or you can have the checks just signed over to us, but we won't take the lump sum." I read those documents pretty carefully. I don't think I would change my mind on that. I don't see how the petitioner is going to gain anything by having a decision come out from me on this.* [**Tr** 214:3-19; 217:3-6.] [Tr = Transcript; 214 = page number; 3-19 = line numbers.]

The above statement by the judge comprises an **oral decision** "from the bench." It carries the same judicial weight as any written decision from the court. The effect was that the petitioner, unless he particularly wanted to go to the added cost of appealing the bench decision, had no choice but to concede the issue.

The judge's position was that the petitioner would have to collect 12 monthly checks of $439 each from Social Security for 16.8 years (his actuarial life expectancy in 1981), and give them all back to the Social Security Trust Fund (from which they came), to constitute a deductible gift. This meant 200 separate monthly gifts over the petitioner's lifetime. This would have caused 200 bureaucratic snafus. The end total would come to $88,583 — the very same figure used by the petitioner on Schedule A of his 1981 return. One — one lifetime gift — would seem to have been the better way. So much for judicial logic.

8

AT TRIAL: ISSUE II

Issue II Addresses Sec. 174(a) Of The IR Code Re The Deductibility Of Certain Expenditures For Developing A 25-Volume Series Of Allyear Tax Books. The "End Product" Of Each Volume Was To Be A Computer Disk Containing All Information In COMPLETE PRE-PRESS BOOK FORM For Instant Publishing. The Expenditures Were For Preparation And Printing Of Hard-Copy DEMONSTRATION SAMPLES In Three Separate Phases. The IRS Argues Against Sec. 174 Under Three Alternate Theories, Namely: 183 (Not For Profit), 263 (Full Capitalization), And 280 (Projected Income). What Does "Experimental" Mean?

In this chapter, the focus is on Issue II: Prototype Expenses. Issue II affects years 1981-83 and 1985-86. Because of the "gap year" 1984, there were actually two separate trials on this issue. There was Trial I (March 1989) and Trial II (December 1989), each presided over by a different judge.

Issue II, as you understand it, addresses petitioner's Schedules C: Profit or Loss From Business or Profession, for the years at issue. On these schedules, petitioner claimed that certain segregated expenditures were for the development of a new series of tax books. The dollar amounts entered were not in question, as they were all verified by invoices and cancelled checks. Both parties stipulated as to their correctness. Thus, the dollar amounts themselves are not in dispute. The issue to be decided is whether the expenditures are allowable as "experimental expenditures" in whole, in part, or not at all.

Issue II adds a new dimension to the IRS's craftiness: the use of *multiple alternative theories* to get its way. As to this issue, **three** different tax theories were presented to the court to convince it that the petitioner was wrong, and the IRS was right. This is an unfair practice because, for each alternate theory, the IRS is presumed correct. The petitioner has to overcome each one separately. The Tax Court treats all IRS theories as viable alternatives to whatever the petitioner may have relied on.

"Sec. 174(a)" Notations on Returns

You have before you not only the trial memorandums, but also the actual tax returns — Forms 1040 and the attached Schedules C — which the petitioner filed with the IRS. If you separate out the Schedules C for each of the five years, you will find that each disputed entry has the hand-entered notation: *Sec. 174(a)*. This is the specific section of the IR Code on which the petitioner relies for claiming his business deductions. The years and amounts in dispute are as follows:

1981	—	$ 47,868)	
1982	—	8,282)	Trial I
1983	—	51,841)	
1985	—	46,535)	
1986	—	13,712)	Trial II
		$168,238	

As you can see, these are substantial amounts. The petitioner is not going to back down simply because the IRS "switches its theories around" to deny various kinds of business deductions.

Since the petitioner specifically identified the disputed entries on each of his Schedules C with the notation "Sec. 174(a)," you take it upon yourself to preview this section on your own. You find that this tax code subsection reads in general part as—

*A taxpayer **may treat** research or **experimental expenditures** which are paid or incurred by him during the taxable year **in connection with** his trade or business as* *expenses which are not chargeable to capital account. The expenditures so treated shall be allowed as a deduction.* [Emphasis added.]

We are citing this subsection for you now because, as the dialogue below will show, the two TC judges actually hearing the case did not review this tax section on their own. They were more interested in the IRS's alternate theories. The point here is that, although TC judges are indeed "tax specialists," they — like everyone else — have blind spots and limitations in their depth of tax knowledge.

Alternate Theories by IRS

Before we get into the trial testimony on Issue II, we need to give you additional tax code background. Otherwise, you'll be hopelessly lost as to what each side is getting at.

As you can surmise from the above, Section 174(a) addresses "experimental expenditures" and says that, if they are "in connection with" a taxpayer's trade or business, they are deductible in the year paid. This seems pretty clear enough. But the IRS can assert that the expenditures are not experimental and thereupon invoke its alternate theories.

From the trial memorandums and procedural discussion with both attorneys, it is evident to you (now) that the alternative tax theories posed by the IRS are:

Theory 1 — **Sec. 183**: Activities not engaged in for profit
☐ Expenses cannot exceed the actual income derived each year.

Theory 2 — **Sec. 263**: Capital expenditures
☐ No deduction (whatsoever) until project abandoned or sold.

Theory 3 — **Sec. 280**: Certain expenditures incurred in production of films, books, or records
☐ Expenses deductible over "projected income stream" of production quantities.

We're not going to quote for you the full statutory wording of these three tax code sections. They'll only confuse you at this point. We've given you the official titles and the gist of their coverage. The point we want you to keep in mind is this: as the IRS hammers away at the witness, it will be "skipping around" among these theories. Our forewarning is to assist you in segregating the fundamental facts on which a decision is to be based.

There is only one witness to testify regarding Issue II. This is the petitioner himself. He prepared all of the Schedules C for the at-issue years, and incurred all of the expenditures in dispute. Consequently, we need make no distinction between WITNESS (P) and WITNESS (R) as we did in Issue I. We'll continue to use the term PETITIONER to signify the petitioner's attorney, in contrast to the petitioner as a witness.

Introduction of Witness

After discussing procedural matters, stipulations as to exhibits, and the scope of Issue II, the following remarks ("blended" between Trials I and II) took place—

THE COURT: All right. You've both waived opening statements. Are you now ready to go ahead with the witness?
PETITIONER: Yes, Your Honor. I'd like to call the petitioner, Mr. _____.
THE COURT: Go ahead.
THE CLERK: Please raise your right hand. [Whereupon the witness was duly sworn.] Be seated. State your name and address for the record. [These were so stated.]

PETITIONER: As I understand it, you are a tax preparer?
WITNESS: That's correct, yes.
Q: When did you become a tax preparer?
A: 1972.
Q: Before becoming a tax preparer, what was your basis work experience?
A: I had 18 years as a technical writer and research engineer with various aerospace and electronic firms. I was primarily a proposal writer in new product development. New ideas would come from different departments of the companies, and formal presentations to customers would have to be made. Once a proposal was accepted and funded, we'd have to proceed to develop it. We continued it as

a development project until it reached fruition, or else just abandon that idea and go on to something else.

Q: And how did it happen that you had this career change?
A: I was unemployed for the entire year of 1971 due to a massive layoff by my last employer. Over the prior 18 years, I was laid off about five times. I was getting tired of this. During 1971 I saw an ad in a newspaper about becoming a tax preparer, after taking some special tax courses. I took the courses, then studied for and took the enrollment exam for license to practice before the IRS.

Q: Now, one of the issues in this case, Mr. _____, is some expenses that you treated as being research and experimental expenses. Are you aware of this?
A: Yes, I am.
Q: What were these expenses related to -- what kind of project?
A: I called the project: **Allyear Tax Guides**. This was a proposed series of 25 new-type tax books.

> *Editorial Note*: See Figure 8.1. Although this exhibit was introduced as demonstrative evidence, the IRS objected because 25 different books had not yet been produced.

The "Project" Described

Petitioner's attorney continued with his direct examination of the witness—

Q: To refresh your memory, in case you need to, could you refer to your 1981 Schedule C?
A: Yes, Schedule C. Right.
Q: Are there some expenses there that refer to "prototype"?
A: Yes, there are: line 31 and some of the sublines thereof.
Q: What are these expenses for?
A: Well, they're for the development of a whole new series of tax books that were slanted or hoped to be slanted to professional level taxpayers. What I was trying to do was to come up with a framework for a 25-volume series somewhere between the professional tax services which come out weekly and the once-a-year tax books that come out at tax time. My goal was to formulate a framework from which some commercial publisher could take on the project and publish my books.

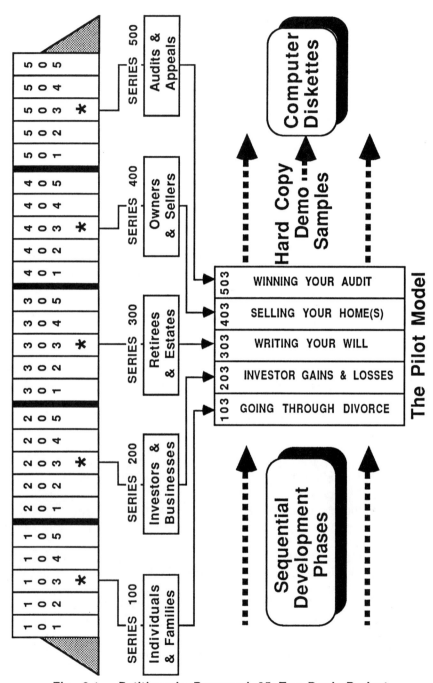

Fig. 8.1 - Petitioner's Proposed 25 Tax Book Project

Now, in order to do that, a number of problems were facing me. In the first place, I had to have some demonstration samples. I needed some kind of samples to test readers -- and publishers -- to find out if this idea was any good. Remember, the idea was to involve 25 different book titles (subjects). So, I had to pick two or three subject titles in order to prepare and print some samples for people to use and refer to.

I got a lot of feedback from these samples, which have since been destroyed. There was no way that I could have undertaken to come up with the end product that I had in mind, which was a computer floppy disk for each tax book that I would write. I tried everything I could to avoid putting this amount of expenditure into this project, but it was necessary that I produce something -- some hard copy samples -- that people could look at and criticize and so forth. I had to demonstrate that I could write multiple books.

Q: Well, in seeking to get this idea off the ground, what, if any, economic considerations did you look into?

A: The basic economic consideration was the production cost of each book. Having done this on my own, going through the whole stage of galley proofs and editing and the graphics and the book design and the photoplates, I found it very costly. So then I evolved more into desktop publishing, whereby my wife and I and daughter actually went ahead and created a fully complete, ready-to-print book, on a computer disk. I have a sample of one of my complete book disks here.

THE COURT: Now, **wait just a moment!** [Emphasis added.]

"Flap" Over Exhibits

At this point, the witness abruptly ceased his testimony. It became quite evident that the judge was mixed up and confused over the stack of stipulated exhibits that the IRS had shoved in.

THE COURT: Let me ask you something. I see this attachment here to your -- what is this, your '81 return.

WITNESS: Yes, there are several attachments to my '81 return.

THE COURT: Yes, but I don't see all of your Schedule C. I see a part of it with depreciation on it.

WITNESS: There's a Schedule C here, Your Honor.

THE COURT: Well, maybe you can find it in my copy.

WITNESS: It isn't there.

THE COURT: I didn't see it either.

PETITIONER: There's been a tremendous problem with so many exhibits, Your Honor.

THE COURT: That's why I look at them and try to find out if I'm missing something.

WITNESS: It is not here, Your Honor. It's not in your copy.

THE COURT: Well, do you all want to correct the Court's copy of Exhibit 5-E?

PETITIONER: Certainly. Also, Your Honor, I'd like to use a demonstrative exhibit, of which I've sent the respondent a reduced-size photocopy. [See Figure 8.2.]

THE COURT: Yes, go ahead and put it [a 2 ft x 3 ft poster] where he [the witness] can see it.

THE IRS: Your Honor, it should be noted for the record that the Respondent has not seen this type of spreadsheet before.

THE COURT: Well, I think he's just going to use it to refresh his recollections.

PETITIONER: Mr._____, I think we were talking about the cost problems in marketing the type of 25-volume series of tax books that you had in mind. You can stand up. No, I guess you can't because you're not recorded.

THE COURT: You've got to be near that [pointing to the microphone].

WITNESS: All right. The first problem I could see is that the tax law is not like literary or artistic prose. You can't print two or three hundred thousand copies of a tax book in one year, and reprint them over a five- or ten-year period. With each book in my proposed series, the shelf life of each title would be no more than about three years. So I had to develop a very economic way of producing a reproducible master copy of each book. This is where the computer floppy disk comes in.

PETITIONER: Your Honor, if you don't mind, maybe I could just move the easel closer to the witness.

THE COURT: Yes, move it over kind of in front of this table so everybody can see it. No, wait a minute. You've got to let the Government Counsel see it, too. Can you see it all right?

THE IRS: I can't read the titles, Your Honor.

THE COURT: Well, I can't read them very well either, even here. I can see "Typical Author" over there and read that.

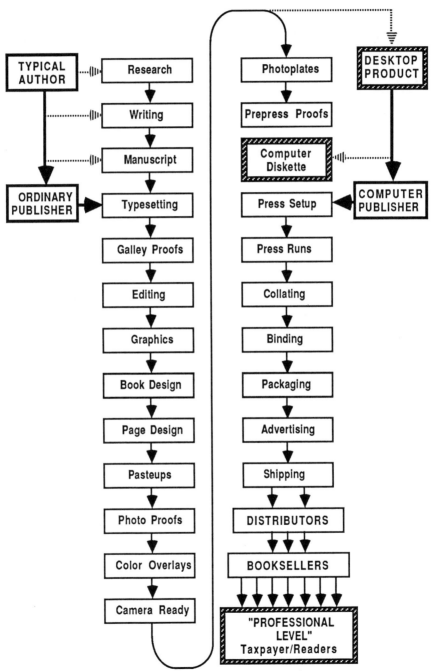

Fig. 8.2 - Necessary Steps in Preparing and Publishing a Book

THE IRS: Is there a document or something that the Petitioner could furnish the Court and the Respondent?
THE COURT: Well, come on up closer and read them. Let's get on with this.

Is Witness a "Typical Author"?

The Court then directed the witness: "Now, go ahead."

WITNESS: All right. Anyhow, the typical author just does the research and writing and prepares a manuscript and sends it to a publisher.
THE IRS: Objection, Your Honor. I don't see how the witness is an expert on what a typical author does.
THE COURT: Well, I don't think he is either, but [to the witness] that was your idea of what he did.
WITNESS: My idea is that I've written two prior technical books (nontax) and I've written these three tax books which are involved in this issue here.
THE COURT: Well, at least that's what you did if you were typical. Go ahead.
WITNESS: When an author goes to a publisher and his manuscript is accepted, the publisher has to go through a whole sequence of events. He's got to go to a typesetter, get it typeset. He's got to print out galley proofs. The galley proofs have to be edited. After the editing is done, he's got to go and intersperse graphics into it.

Then there's a page design to be done. Each page in the book has to be laid out and designed. It's not something that happens on its own. Then you take the edited proofs and the graphics which have been edited and intersperse them into a pasteup onto one page at a time on the book.

After the pasteups, you go and have them photocopied to prove out the book. And, again, you go back and do editing, and then bring in your color overlays. These have to be pasted on and overlaid on the particular area that you want to color emphasize.

Then you go on from that point into making up camera-ready proofs, again to recheck everything before you go into the next phase -- which has to do with photoplates before they go onto the press. Then you have to touch up all the negatives for the photoplates, then run a prepress proof of **all** the pages in the book called "blue lines." Then you have to go through all the blue lines for more editing. Every time you do another step in the process, you introduce errors into it.

And so I said to myself, "Hey, I can do all this through my desktop computer, and create a **complete** book on a disk -- formatted in all respects -- and send it to the publisher direct. Depending on how computer modernized he is, he can eliminate all of these steps that I've been talking about. Much publishing time and money could be saved.

Now, unfortunately, when thinking of a new series of 25 tax books, I've got to formulate a standard text design, both from the point of view of editorial consistency and from the point of view of production consistency. So the expenditures I incurred were getting the experience so that I could standardize things. After all, when you're starting anything new, you never succeed the first time you try. It takes time. I've been in programs that have taken 15 to 20 years developing new products and new concepts -- the big payoff just doesn't come overnight.

THE IRS: Objection, Your Honor. I don't see how this is relevant to our proceedings.

THE COURT: Well, I think he's going past the question anyhow.

Back to the Tax Issue

Petitioner's attorney picked up the "hint" from the Court that the testimony was veering away from the basic tax dispute on the various Schedules C by the witness. To refocus the testimony, the petitioner's attorney continued his direct examination as follows—

PETITIONER: Now, the prototype expenses you show on your 1981 return, what specifically are they for?

WITNESS: They are for the preparation and printing of hard-copy **samples** of my proposed tax books.

Q: Now, the prototype expenses on your '82, '83, '85, and '86 returns -- are they for the same kind of book samples?

A: Yes, they're all demonstration samples for sending to prospective publishers and reviewers.

Q: Were they all printed at the same time, or were they printed in phases or batches?

A: They were printed in phases. Phase I was '81; Phase II was '83; and Phase III was '85. There were some "spillover" expenses in '82, '84, and '86. As each new phase was printed, any remaining samples from the predecessor phase were destroyed.

Q: Why was it necessary to print the samples in different phases?
A: As I got feedback from publishers and reviewers, I changed things: formatting, subject depth, diagrams, chapter arrangements, and so on. Also, 1981 through 1986 was a period of a lot of tax law changes, and this made it difficult to keep the subject titles updated.
Q: In Phase III, how many book titles did you print?
A: There were five separate book titles, of 100 copies each. They were quite expensive, but I felt that I had to do it.
Q: Now, in what way, if any, was this third printing different from the second printing that you had done?
A: Well, the third printing -- Phase III, that is -- was in looseleaf form -- three-ring looseleaf binding for updating. The second thing is that each chapter was separately paginated. This way, if there's some change in the law that affected one chapter, I didn't have to go through the whole book and redo the whole thing over again.
    The third thing was, I used what I call "color emphasized" text. I put color into the text so that persons could skim-read a book by just reading the color parts and omitting the other parts. The problem with tax books is that they tend to be dull and I'm trying to induce people to read only those subject matters which are of most interest to them.
PETITIONER: That's all the testimony I have.
THE COURT: Respondent, you may cross-examine.
THE IRS: Thank you, Your Honor.
WITNESS: May I set all these exhibits and samples aside, because it's crowded here?

Were Printed Samples Necessary?

Now comes the IRS with its cross-examination of the witness. Accordingly, the following testimony ensued.

THE IRS: At the time you started this series, did you know that changes in the tax law would adversely affect the project?
WITNESS: Yes, I knew it and I was concerned about it.
Q: If you knew it, why did you publish the books, if you knew they were going to be obsolete?
A: Otherwise, I'd have nothing to show as a demonstration sample. I can't just talk words. I had to have some hard-copy end product to show the type of 25-book series that I had in mind.

Q: So you published these books knowing they would be obsolete?
A: Yes.
Q: Is it possible to get a book published without actually printing it yourself?
A: Yes, one book -- but not a proposed series of 25 books.
Q: The letters that you wrote to publishers that are attached as Joint Exhibit 10-J and the replies -- do you recall those letters?
A: Yes, not a particular one that you might be reading but the general series, yes.
Q: Did you write those letters to obtain financial backing?
A: Yes, I did.
THE COURT: And I take it nobody would back it?
WITNESS: Yes, because it hadn't been developed enough to the stage where there was commercial interest in it.
THE IRS: When this book was published, say, by a commercial publisher, would they be able to utilize all of your developments?
A: You say a book. I'm talking a series of books.
Q: Yes, a series.
A: We are also talking one computer disk for each book, okay? Each computer disk -- in **complete book form**: NOT manuscript form -- could go directly to a publisher's printer/binder, as I indicated on that poster over there [Figure 8.2].
Q: Did any of those letters of Joint Exhibit 10-J tell you that you had to have actual demonstration samples?
A: No, because they--
Q: No?
A: No, because they like to see samples to use for cost estimating purposes.
Q: But your answer is no.
A: No, the letters didn't direct me to have them, no.

IRS: Still "Hammering Away"

Continuing with its cross-examination, the IRS's attorney presses hard against the witness. The testimony continues—

THE IRS: You testified earlier that this series that you had in mind consisted basically of three prototypes; is that correct?
A: No, I didn't testify to that. I said I have a series of 25 books in mind.

Q: No, let me explain my question. You went through, in a sense, three revisions of this idea.
A: Oh, three **phases**, yes.

Q: Now the invoices [which are among the exhibits] for tax years 1981 through 1983, do they relate to phases one and two?
A: That's correct, yes.
Q: And what's at issue here, in 1985 and 1986, is phase three? Is that true?
A: Phase three, and a partial transition to phase four--
Q: Oh, so there's a phase four?
A: Phase four is each book in complete **press-ready** form on a computer disk. We've already mentioned this as the "end product" of my desktop publishing effort.

THE IRS: The witness has now testified as to the invoices on phases one and two of his textbook project. What we are referring to here is phase three. So I would like to move to exclude Joint Exhibits 1-A through 10-J from the record in this case.
THE COURT: Objection overruled.
THE IRS: These samples, or rough copies as you call them, were actually printed books, correct?
A: Yes, that's right.
Q: They were books that are common as a book on a normal book shelf?
A: In that respect they were common, but not as far as content. They deal with tax matters which change frequently.

Q: The descriptions on these invoices show various costs. Are these costs normal recurring costs, when one goes to print a book -- any book?
A: To print any book, one has to engage in typesetting, the page layouts, the graphics. If that's your question, yes-- but--
Q: That is my question.
A: But as far as "recurring," I have difficulty with that. If one has to reprint a book for updating, then there're changes -- all changes introduce errors which means that you have to recheck everything all over again.
Q: It's possible to retain what's called "camera-ready" art for making additional printings; is that true?
A: If there were no changes, that could be true, yes.
Q: That was my hypothetical.

A: Yeah, most hypothetical. You obviously have had no experience with tax book publishing, editing, and updating.

Are Computer Disks Software?

Still continuing its cross-examination process, the IRS asks the witness:

Q: Mr. _____, those expenses that are shown on your invoices from various companies, are they of a kind that are normally incurred by an author?
A: Not normally, no.
Q: You also testified that you were reducing your manuscripts to a computer device?
A: Yes.

Q: And were you developing computer software programs?
A: Each disk could be construed as a software program. Each disk contains all the information necessary for printing a complete book. Each disk would go to a publisher who had a computer-directed press. There would be no intermediate steps in between. It would be a one-step process from author to a printing press.
Q: Would the software controlling the functions of getting these volumes into press--would that be in the hands of an outside printer, or yourself?
A: Well, he would have both. He would have my disk, and he would have his own programs that would internally direct the printing run.

Q: But the disk that held your supposed book -- was it not basically a manuscript reduced to a disk?
A: It was more than that. It contained the complete book with nothing further necessary for the publisher to do -- press-preparation-wise, that is. All of those preparatory steps that I'd been talking about on my display chart over there [Figure 8.2], I have done as the author.
I shortcutted a lot of the press-preparation steps on my computer disks. I went from the manuscript, to the page layouts, to the illustrations, to the pagination, the contents, title page -- the whole works. So all a publisher would have to do is take my disk, put it into his printing press, and then, on a separate press, go put his cover on.

Q: But this was all typed in by you on your home computer, is that correct?

A: Yes, I have a computer/printer setup: a complete "desktop publishing" arrangement. When I'm all through each disk, it is a complete book in **press-ready** form.

Q: So each of your disks is a substitute for a stack of paper that was camera-ready art?

A: It was an advancement over that --

Q: Only that it was a computer disk, versus hard copy?

A: It was far more than that. I took it upon myself to help get these books out so that they could be published on an economical basis -- because of the updating problem with tax matters.

THE IRS: Nothing further, Your Honor.

THE COURT: Any redirect?

PETITIONER: Not on this issue, Your Honor.

THE COURT: Anything else?

THE IRS: No, Your Honor.

THE COURT: Well, there's one thing I wanted to ask both of you, and that is I gather in the so-called development expenses, it is mainly an issue of whether they are deductible research and development expenses under Section 174 or whether they are capitalized expenditures in connection with a literary or artistic production under other sections of the Code, such as 183, 263, or 280. Is that the main issue here?

PETITIONER: Your Honor, what we're really talking about is whether it's in connection with the petitioner's trade or business; that is, whether it's a 162 or a 174 deduction.

THE COURT: It's just a question. I've got to have briefs about the claimed research and development expenses. I did read this 280 and it does say "book"; it doesn't say "literary work." I'm not sure whether the testimony was to develop a book or a series of books.

9

AT TRIAL: ISSUE III

Issue III Addresses (Former) Sec. 6653(b) Of The IR Code Re Applicability Of The Civil Fraud Penalty Against Petitioner (H) For Renouncing His Lifetime Social Security Benefits And Discontinuing The Social Security Self-Employment Tax. Separately, His Spouse Was Also Charged With Fraud. Although Petitioner Could Show Substantial Savings To The U.S. Treasury (EXHIBIT 30-AD), The IRS Argued That The Idea Was So "Outrageous, Preposterous, And Frivolous" That The CRIMINAL Fraud Penalty Was Also Considered (EXHIBIT 59-BG). All "Badges Of Fraud" Must Relate To Intent To Evade Tax.

This time, it's a BIG ONE! It is Issue III: Fraud Penalty. This is a penalty (at the time) of 50% of the total amount of any deficiency asserted by the IRS. It applies to each "carryover" year identified with the initial fraudulent act.

Editorial Note: The fraud penalty statute — formerly Code Sec. 6653(b) — has been amended several times since the years at issue herein. It has been increased to 75% and renumbered as Code Sec. 6663. We'll comment further on this new penalty in Chapter 12.

Issue III affects all years 1981 through 1986: a total of six years. Although 1984 was a "closed year" (no deficiency asserted, initially), the IRS can open it up if it can establish that there was any *taint* of fraud committed immediately before or immediately after

1984. Any tainting is automatically construed by the IRS as willful intent to evade tax.

As in Issue II, there were two trials for Issue III. The transcripted testimony is essentially the same for both trials (though before different TC judges). This is because the alleged fraudulent act was committed in 1981 and taintedly carried over into the subsequent years. However, Trial II exposes a novel switch in the IRS's penalty tactics and really gets to the bottom of why fraud was asserted. It all comes out when IRS Agent No. 2 finally discloses his "proof."

As to this issue, four witnesses will testify. There will be two witnesses for the petitioner and two witnesses for the IRS. We'll designate them as WITNESS (P1) and WITNESS (P2) for the petitioner, and as WITNESS (R1) and WITNESS (R2) for the respondent.

Unless you have previously ordered other trial transcripts from the Tax Court, you'll not find in any other tax book the actual testimony of two IRS agents under oath. Thus, you are being treated to a rare insight into the working practices of IRS bureaucracy. These disclosures will give you precious knowledge which few of your peers will ever possess.

The Judicial "Badges of Fraud"

For background purposes, you need to know the elements that constitute fraud, as decided by other judges in the past. Suprisingly, these elements are **not prescribed** in the IR Code nor by IRS/Treasury Regulations. Yet, you need to know the "badges of fraud" for making an objective decision on your own.

The earliest tax fraud case on record apparently took place in 1926. This is the case of *Swartz & Co., Inc. vs IRS*, 5 BTA 264(A). [The "BTA" is Board of Tax Appeals, predecessor to the Tax Court.] The BTA court held that before fraud can be asserted, the taxpayer's conduct must be characterized by: (1) bad faith; and (2) intent to evade tax.

Even as late as 1983 [*Schmitz, J.N. vs IRS*, TC Memo 1983-482], the Tax Court set out three elements of fraud as being: (1) a knowing falsehood; (2) an underpayment of tax; and (3) an intent to evade tax. These characterizing elements were further upheld in 1986 [*Regan, S.K. vs IRS*, TC Memo 1986-120] when the Tax Court ruled against the IRS saying—

There was no bad faith, intentional wrongdoing, sinister motive, or intent to mislead or deceive the IRS where taxpayers timely filed returns that set forth clearly their deductions . . . even though they were annoyed with government.

Between 1926 and 1986, there are well over 1,000 documented TC cases involving the assertion of fraud by the IRS. Out of this vast reservoir of judicial wisdom, certain clear and unmistakable **badges of fraud** flash through. Why hasn't the IRS assimilated these "badges" to guide its own agents, as well as guiding the taxpaying public?
We'll tell you why.
Because the IRS loses about two out of every three fraud cases: about 65%. It wants to keep its public image alive that it always wins. If it were to outline in Treasury Regulations the essential elements constituting fraud, it would be a public admission that it does not always win. Furthermore, if the IRS were to outline the judicially-accepted badges of fraud in its regulations, and some IRS agent or agents violated the fraud regulations, the wronged taxpayer would have a legal cause of action against such agent or agents in Federal District Courts. The IRS just can't take the heat of being on the losing side of a fraud issue.
Yet, the IRS does win in approximately 35% of its fraud cases. As every TC judge knows, one cannot use statistical probabilities when rendering a decision concerning fraud. One needs competent guidelines which neither the IR Code nor IRS Regulations provides.
In 1987 (**prior** to Trials I and II on Issue III herein), the Ninth Circuit Federal Court of Appeals issued a 6-point edict on the elements of fraud. It identified certain types of circumstantial evidence from which fraudulent intent may be inferred. It specifically identified the "badges of fraud" as—

1. **Understatement of income**
2. **Inadequate records**
3. **Failure to file tax returns**
4. **Implausible or inconsistent explanation**
5. **Concealment of assets**
6. **Failure to cooperate with tax agents**

[Citation from *Edelson vs IRS*, 829 F. 2nd 828,832.]

We urge you to keep these six indices in mind as you weigh the testimony and evidence below. You must not be persuaded by *implications* of fraud, no matter how credible they may otherwise appear.

Self-Employment Social Security

Petitioner (H), husband, had been previously sworn before the court when testifying on Issues I and II. He thus continued under oath on the witness stand for Issue III. This time, however, for differentiation of testimony, he is designated as WITNESS (P1): first petitioner's witness. Since the burden of proof of fraud is on the IRS, the petitioner's attorney need only elicit testimony that plausibly explains those acts which he anticipates the IRS will target as fraud. This part of the testimony is culled primarily from the Trial I transcript.

PETITIONER (attorney): You are a tax preparer; is that correct?
WITNESS (P1): Yes, that's correct. I'm self-employed.
Q: When did you become a self-employed tax-preparer?
A: 1972
Q: Prior to that time, had you any experience in tax preparation?
A: Not directly in tax preparation, no.
Q: Did you have any experience in other areas of taxes?
A: Yes, tax reform, property tax reform particularly. I formed a group called United Taxpayers of Santa Clara County. I became the first president of it. We were instrumental in seeking property tax relief for the whole state of California. We helped to sponsor Proposition 13 which finally passed in 1978.

Q: Do you have before you Exhibit 22-V, the letter you sent to President Reagan on May 12, 1981?
A: Yes, I have it.
Q: What was the purpose in sending this letter?
A: It was two-fold. One purpose was to renounce my lifetime Social Security benefits as a public gift to those in greater need [Issue I]. The second purpose was to decline making further self-employment Social Security tax payments, inasmuch as I would never be able to collect my benefits, by virtue of my irrevocable renunciation.
Q: Now, had you had occasion, prior to this letter to the President, to consider some of the problems of Social Security?

A: Yes. Previously, in about 1975, I applied for an exemption from the self-employment tax, and agreed to waive forever all of my lifetime Social Security benefits. The Social Security system seemed to be perpetually underfunded in those days, and the best way to strengthen it, I thought, was to cut down on the number of persons collecting lifetime benefits.

Q: So, you had some political opinions as to the inclusion of self-employed persons in Social Security?
A: Yes, I became philosophically opposed to Social Security once I became self-employed and learned that for the first 20 years of the Social Security system, it did not apply to self-employed persons.

While doing tax work, many of my clients who were self-employed would raise the question: "Why do we have to pay this? We can take care of ourselves." This coincided with my own personal feeling that if you were self-employed and could take care of yourself, there's no reason to have the Government take care of you. Presumably, that's why there's a special tax form for application for exemption.

Form 4029 Application Denied

Continuing with the line of direct examination above—

Q: You mentioned previously that you sought to exempt yourself from Social Security?
A: Yes, I did.
Q: Can you tell the Court as briefly as possible the procedures that you took?

A: Yes, there's an established form, a **Form 4029**. It is an application for exemption from Social Security tax on self-employment income and the waiver of all benefits from the Social Security system. I did file this form properly, timely, and I set forth my reasons. I was in conscientious opposition to collecting Social Security based on the fact that I could take care of myself in my old age, and on the fact that I was getting a military retirement and I would have no need for Social Security.

Q: Did you pursue the matter any further than filing the exemption form?

A: Yes, the exemption was denied. And, since I had already paid some of the self-employment tax anyhow, I pursued the matter into District Court and again into Appeals Court.
Q: Did you represent yourself?
A: Yes, I represented myself all the way into Appeals Court. I made my own oral argument before a three-judge panel there.
Q: I take it that you didn't prevail or we wouldn't be here today?
A: Obviously not.

Code Section 1404 Proposed

Further continuing with the line of direct examination above—

Q: Do you recall receiving Exhibit 25-Y, dated June 18, 1981 from the Commissioner of Social Security?
A: Yes, I received that letter from him.
Q: And in response, did you send Exhibit 30-AD?
A: Yes, that's the letter that I responded to the Commissioner of Social Security on July 2nd.
Q: What was the purpose in sending the letter of July 2nd to the Commissioner?

A: He had mentioned in his letter of June 18th Sections 1402(g) and (h) of the Internal Revenue Code which had to do with exemptions of self-employed persons from Social Security. Since I had tried those code sections previously, I proposed to him a new code section to take into account the renunciatory procedure, the one that I used, to encourage other self-employed persons to do the same. I mentioned that there would be great savings to the Treasury Department. I even quoted and showed the computations for a potential 5-year budget saving of 16 billion dollars if the Government would enact this idea. I based my estimated savings to the U.S. Treasury on only 1% of those persons in the age span of 62-65 renouncing their Social Security benefits.

Q: There was an attachment to Exhibit 30-AD; is that correct?
A: Yes, there was an attachment. I called it Section 1404: Deductions for Irrevocable Renunciation of Social Security Benefits. It was a proposal to amend the Internal Revenue Code, the portion dealing with tax on self-employment income.

Editorial Note: See highlights of this proposal in Figure 9.1.

Q: Without going into details, because the Judge can read your letter and its attachment later, was it a new statute that you hoped that the Commissioner would at least consider for reform in Social Security?
A: Yes, it certainly was.

Q: Did you pay any self-employment Social Security tax on Schedules SE, I believe, for 1981, '82, and '83?
A: Initially, no. Subsequently, yes. I took the Schedules SE matter separately into Federal District Court in June 1986. A decision was rendered against me in April 1987. So then I amended my Schedules SE and paid the self-employment tax.
Q: Nothing further, Your Honor.

Now, The IRS's Turn

In cross-examination, where the IRS has the burden of proof, it is not limited to the direct testimony of the witness on the stand. It can branch off into many areas to establish, circumstantially, a "state of mind" of intent to evade tax. The state-of-mind search is not limited to the particular tax years at issue. On this basis, then, the IRS's attorney proceeded to home in on the witness.

THE IRS: Did you receive Exhibit 25-Y from the Commissioner of Social Security?
WITNESS (P1):   Yes, I received that.
Q: Could you read for me the second paragraph in the first sentence?
A: "There are no provisions in the Social Security law which permit an individual to voluntarily withdraw from the Social Security system."
Q: Could you look at Exhibit 30-AD, and read the third paragraph, first sentence, please?
A: "I've been philosophically opposed to the Social Security Act from its inception."

Q: Did you send a copy of these letters, any one of them, to the Internal Revenue Service?

PETITIONER'S BUSINESS LETTERHEAD

TO -
- Commissioner, Social Security
- Secretary, Health & Welfare

July 2, 1981

Internal Revenue Code
Chapter 2 - TAX ON SELF-EMPLOYMENT INCOME

■ Sec. 1401 - Rate of Tax   ■ Sec. 1402 - Deductions   ■ Sec. 1403 - Misc. Provisions

Sec. 1404 - Deductions for Irrevocable Renunciation of Social Security Benefits

(a) **General rule**
— Having attained age 62 - 65, eligible to commence receiving Social Security benefits, may elect to irrevocably renounce them ....

(b) **Verification of alternative plan**
— Electee must provide evidence of an alternative plan at least equivalent to Social Security ....

(c) **Recapture of contributions**
— Upon verification by Commissioner of Social Security, recapture amount indexed by CPI ....

(d) **Charitable deduction for beneficial rights**
— Excess of actuarial entitlement over adjusted contributions, deductible as a public gift ....

(e) **Waiver forever of all benefits**
— Shall waive forever all benefits and other payments under the Social Security Act ....

(f) **Subsequent exemption from Sec. 1401**
— Any election under subsec. (a), shall exempt electee from all Social Security taxes thereafter ....

ESTIMATED 5-Year Savings to U.S. Treasury

- Approx. 6,300,000 beneficiaries age 62 - 65.
- Average lifetime payout: $113,682 per beneficiary.
- **If only 1% were to renounce -**

  ☐ 1st-yr savings: $113,682 x 63,000 = 7.16 billion
  ☐ 2nd -5th-yr: $113,682 x 84,000 * = 9.55 billion

* Approx. 2,100,000 NEW CLAIMANTS age 62 - 65 each year x 4 years

$16.71 BILLION

Fig. 9.1 - Key Excerpts from Petitioner's EXHIBIT 30-AD

A : No, but I asked in my last paragraph to the President that he instruct and have the Internal Revenue Service get in touch with me on procedures on how to pursue -- with this renunciation idea of mine.

Q : Did you ask the IRS at the time you were contemplating these deductions for a private letter ruling concerning the propriety of this deduction?

A : It wouldn't have done any good if I'd have asked them, but I did not ask them.

Q : I'd like you at this time to look at Exhibit 34-AH.

A : Yes. [September 15, 1981]

Q : Is this in response to your letter that was forwarded on your behalf from Congressman Mineta?

A : No, there are several letters here. I wrote to Secretary Schweiker on May 22nd [1981] and it appears to me that this is in response to that letter. In my May 22nd letter, I attached a copy of my proposed new tax code section.

Q : Can you read the first sentence of the second paragraph of Exhibit 34-AH?

A : "We have received your proposal and we regret that we cannot endorse it."

Q : At the time you received this letter from Secretary Schweiker, did you forward a copy to the Internal Revenue Service?

A : No, because he said he was going to do it. The very last sentence there reads: "I am forwarding a copy of your letter to Secretary of the Treasury, Donald T. Regan."

Q : But you did not do it yourself?

A : Well, he was going to do it.

Q : Is it your testimony that you did send a copy of this letter to the IRS?

A : No, I didn't do it because --

PETITIONER: Your Honor, we're getting argumentative now. He's answered the question.

THE COURT: Go ahead. He said he didn't send a copy to the Internal Revenue Service.

THE IRS: I'd just like it on the record, Your Honor.

The Perjury Knockout

The IRS, further continuing its cross-examination of WITNESS (P1) asked—

Q: You filed a claim for refund of self-employment taxes in 1972 through 1974 in the Federal District Court, is that correct?
A: No, not quite. I paid the tax and filed a refund claim with the IRS and when that was disapproved, I went into District Court.
Q: Was the basis for that refund claim concerning your exemption as a member of the Universal Life Church?
A: Not on the original claim, no.

THE IRS: Your Honor, I'd like to show you and the Petitioner documents that Respondent has obtained from the **archives** of the Federal District Court.
THE COURT: All right.
PETITIONER: Your Honor, are these part of the exhibits that I have seen?
THE COURT: Are they part of the exhibits in evidence?
THE IRS: No, they're not, Your Honor. They're being used to impeach the witness.
THE COURT: All right. Go ahead. Offer it and have it marked.
THE CLERK: This will be Respondent's Exhibit DQ.
THE COURT: Show the witness a copy.
Q: Mr. _____, I'd like to direct your attention towards the back of this group of documents marked Exhibit DQ. It's numbered 89 and it's a Form 4029. Do you recognize this form?
A: Yeah, that's the 4029. I mentioned it earlier; that was the application for exemption that I had submitted.
Q: Do you recognize the following page, which is numbered 91, another 4029?   A: Yes
Q: And can you read the name of the religious group that is typed in?   A: Yes

Q: And now the following page, which is marked 92, does the same name appear there?   A: Yes
Q: So you were associated with the Universal Life Church?
A: No, I wasn't.

> *Editorial Note*: This is a perjurious statement by petitioner (H).
> All Forms 4029 were signed under "penalties of perjury."

Q: These documents claim that you were.
A: Yes, but they were dated 1974, '75, and '76. I got them signed by the ULC Bishop in Modesto because the first application I filed was based on "nonsectarian-independent" religious grounds,

which was summarily disapproved by the IRS. I was told that I had to affiliate with a religious organization in order to file the 4029 exemption claim. I then contacted the Bishop and got his permission to put this name, Universal Life Church, on there. Subsequent to that, I had no further contact with the Universal Life Church.

Q: Now, I'd like to show you a document labeled Number 134; is this in response to your request for information from your Congressman?
A: Yes. Please note that the document you are showing me is dated December **1976**.
Q: I'd like now to direct your attention to Document 123.
A: Yes. That's my letter to my Congressman dated July 1976.
Q: Can you read the first sentence of the second paragraph?
A: "Administratively I have applied four times for exemptions from the payment of self-employment tax, in exchange for waiving all rights of ever receiving any benefits from Social Security." Do you want me to go on?
Q: No, that's fine.

THE IRS: Your Honor, at this time I'd like to move all of these exhibits into evidence.
THE COURT: Well, they were received to impeach the witness. Do you want to put them in for a separate purpose in addition to impeaching him, or for another purpose such as his donative intent?
THE IRS: Yes, Your Honor. He also filed for exemption from the self-employment tax in 1978, which was denied.
THE COURT: Well, it seems to me that he testified that he appealed it.
THE IRS: That's precisely why I'd like to enter this document along with all the others, to show that the appeal was denied. And then he appealed it to the U.S. Supreme Court which also was dismissed.
THE COURT: Well, it wasn't granted. Certiorari wasn't granted.
WITNESS (P1): Yes, Your Honor. Certiorari was denied on October 1, 1979.
THE IRS: No further questions for this witness, Your Honor.

Petitioner's Wife: Witness (P2)

The petitioner's wife was called to testify in her own behalf. As stated before, the IRS had asserted the fraud penalty against her for 1981. She was duly sworn and took the witness stand. Petitioner's attorney began his direct examination of her as follows:

PETITIONER: Mrs. _____, do you have any special education in the area of tax law?
WITNESS (P2):   None whatsoever.
Q: Have you ever prepared tax returns?   A : No.
Q: Do you help your husband in his tax preparation business?
A: Only as backup. He does it our home, so I'm the general factotum, secretary, janitress, and babysitter for clients' children.

Q: Did you sign the 1981 tax return that was filed by yourself and your husband?   A : I did.
Q: When you signed it, did you understand that you were taking a charitable deduction for a contribution to Social Security?
A: Yes, I did.
Q: Would you tell the Court what you understood about that deduction?
A: Well, I had typed the letter to the President, so I knew what my husband was doing. He wanted to renounce and give his lifetime Social Security benefits to the Government. He knew it was a test case and hoped that somebody would see the value in it, because it was a very wonderful idea. It would give the Government a lot of money, and a lot of people perceived this as a good idea, which I agree with.
Q: Did you understand that there was a likelihood that you would be audited?
A: Oh, yes. There was no question.

Q: Let me hand you Exhibit 65-BM (dated March 4, 1985) and Exhibit 66-BN (dated March 27, 1985), and ask if you recognize these documents?   A : Yes, I do.
Q: What was the purpose of 65-BM, which is a letter you wrote to your Congressman, Ed Zschau?
A: Since I thought my husband's renunciation of his Social Security benefits was such a good idea, I wrote to see if maybe someone else that he hadn't been able to reach would pick up on this and see the benefit to the country.

Q: And did you ask your Congressman for some information?

A: Yes. I told him I would like to give up my Social Security and just not accept it, as I was becoming eligible for it very shortly -- at age 65. I thought maybe in this interim between '81 and '85, somebody else may have thought up the idea, and that there might be some clear-cut renunciatory procedures available and for which a charitable deduction would be recognized.

Q: Is Exhibit 66-BN the response that your Congressman sent you in 1985?

A: Yes, and he said he was sending my inquiry to the Social Security Administration and commended me for my efforts.

Q: Were you given anything subsequent to that letter that indicated that you would be able to renounce, as you planned to?

A: Unfortunately, the Social Security Administration did not seem to know how to handle it. Separately, Dan Rostenkowski, Chairman of the Ways and Means Committee in Congress, suggested that I contact the Internal Revenue Service. Well, that was a dead end, because my husband had not been successful in obtaining any regulations from them on the same subject. They seemed to be interested only in applying for benefits, not in renouncing them.

PETITIONER: I have no further questions, Your Honor. The Respondent may cross examine.

Comes, Now, IRS to Attack

The IRS's attorney lost no time in getting into his cross-examination. He jump-started by asking petitioner's wife—

THE IRS: Mrs. _____, did your husband ask if you would renounce your benefits?

WITNESS (P2): No, he did not.

Q: But you did so on that letter to the President dated 1981?

A: I did not renounce my benefits.

Q: Did you renounce any survivorship benefits you may have, based on your husband's contribution to Social Security?

A: The word "survivor benefits" never came up. He renounced his Social Security. If it included my survivor benefits, that was fine with me, but I don't know that it did.

THE COURT: Did your husband consult with you before the May 1981 letter?
WITNESS (P2):   Oh, yes. I typed it. I wouldn't have typed it if I hadn't agreed with it.

THE IRS: Let the record show that I'm furnishing the witness with a copy of Exhibit 70-BR [dated July 9, 1985 by the Commissioner of Social Security].
Q: Mrs. _____, could you read the second and third sentences of the second paragraph for the Court, please.
A: "People who wish to make a financial contribution to the Social Security program may do so. However, only voluntary and unconditional money gifts and bequests can be accepted."

Q: You applied for your benefits in October of 1985, correct?
A: Yes, correct.
Q: And you are currently receiving benefit checks?
A: That's correct.
Q: Did you give those proceeds to the Social Security Trust Fund?
A: No, I did not.
Q: What do you do with the funds; do you deposit them in your joint checking account?
A: Yes, and then I give the money away.
THE COURT: Excuse me, I didn't get the end of that answer.
WITNESS (P2):   After my Social Security benefits are deposited in the bank, I use the money to give away to other people and organizations. I do not use it for my own benefit.
THE COURT: In other words, you make charitable contributions of it to somebody other than the Social Security Administration?
WITNESS (P2):   That's correct.
THE IRS: No further questions, Your Honor.

IRS Witness No. 1:   Auditor

With respect to all facets of Issue III (fraud), the IRS has the burden of proof and eventually has to put its own witnesses on the stand. The usual procedure is for each IRS agent/witness to give a lengthy recitation of his or her background, training, and experience as an IRS employee. This is to show that the witnesses are highly qualified individuals with extensive knowledge in federal tax administration. The IRS needs to do this to protect its "presumption of correctness" image. We'll dispense with most of this background testimony.

> *Editorial Note*: The presumption of correctness theory that favors the IRS does NOT apply to the fraud penalty. It applies only to the "determination" of a tax deficiency which is a prerequisite to the fraud assertion. The IRS cannot assert fraud, then rely on its presumption theory to avoid its burden of proof.

With the above in mind, the IRS's first witness (a female), designated as WITNESS (R1), was duly sworn and took the stand. The IRS's attorney then proceeded with his direct examination:

THE IRS: What was your position in the Internal Revenue Service at the time of your examination of the Petitioners' returns?
WITNESS (R1):   I was a revenue agent in the Compliance Group, San Jose.
Q: At the time of the audit, had you ever heard of Mr. _____ before?
A: No.
Q: Can you define for us the years of the audit examination?
A: Initially, it was for 1981. This was expanded when I sent for the subsequent years, and the '82 turned out to be what we call a TCMP audit. So, we picked up '82 and '83 also.
Q: What's the difference between a TCMP audit versus a normal audit?
A: A TCMP audit is a line-by-line examination for the purpose of determining abusive entries, large deductions, and other things that "stick out" on a return.
Q: What items stuck out on the Petitioners' returns?
A: Specifically, the items that were targeted were the (charitable) contribution deduction on the Schedules A, the prototype expenses on the Schedules C, and the nonpayment of self-employment tax on the Schedules SE.
Q: When did you first meet with the Petitioner?
A: I think it was about June 13th of '84.
Q: Was the Petitioner prepared for your visit?
A: Yes. Mr. _____ is a meticulous individual. He keeps things orderly, in envelopes, and, yes, he was prepared.
Q: How long did that initial visit last?
A: Four to six hours, in through there, time off for lunch.

Q: What was the outcome of your audit examination of the Petitioners' returns for the years at issue?

A: For all three years, I disallowed the Schedule A contributions; I disallowed the Schedule C prototype expenses; and I included the self-employment tax on the Schedules SE.

Section 6653(b) Fraud Asserted

The IRS's attorney continued his direct examination of the witness as follows—

Q: At the time you initially received the file, did you see any documents or any letters that Mr. _____ sent to the Internal Revenue Service?

A: Only his return.

Q: During the audit procedure did he mention his experiences with the Universal Life Church?

A: I can't say he mentioned Universal Life Church specifically. I was aware of that through my own research.

Q: Did he mention any of his prior District Court decisions?

A: He said he had been through the courts before, which of course triggered me to look it all up.

Q: But he didn't specifically mention a Federal District Court; he just said any court or some court?

A: He said he had been through the court system before and was willing to do it again.

Q: Then did you recommend the fraud penalty pursuant to IR Code Section 6653(b)?

A: I did.

Q: Can you give us your reasons for doing so?

PETITIONER: Objection, Your Honor. Obviously her opinion is not relevant. It may be foundational --

THE COURT: Well, it's not taken to influence the Court's opinion. If it's a relevancy objection, I don't know what relevancy; I don't know why she set up that addition to tax. But no matter what, it's not going to affect the Court's decision.

THE IRS: Well, Your Honor, we're not attempting to go behind the statutory notice of deficiency, but just to show the Court that in fact the fraud penalty was included on the revenue agent's report delivered to Mr. _____ in July 1984.

THE COURT: She's already said that, that she recommended.

THE IRS (addressing the witness): Was the civil fraud penalty included on the report that you furnished to Mr. _____?

WITNESS (R1):   I think it was.

PETITIONER: Well, I'll stipulate that it's certainly an issue in this case.

THE IRS: No further questions, Your Honor.

No Unreported Income Found

The petitioner's attorney started right off into his cross-examination by asking the IRS's witness — Agent No. 1 (the auditor) — the following line of questions:

PETITIONER: Ms. _____ , you've testified that Mr. _____ with his 1981 return took this large charitable contribution and did not pay his Social Security self-employment tax. Are these items of the type that are bound to be chosen for possible audit?

WITNESS (R1):   It has a better chance. It doesn't mean that it will be chosen.

Q: But there is a very strong likelihood that it would; isn't that correct?

A: If somebody saw it, they would take a second look at it.

Q: As I understand it, Mr. _____ had everything there that you asked for?

A: That's correct.

Q: And all of the numbers on his return balanced to the penny; isn't that correct?

A: Yeah, within a de minimis amount.

Q: And you found Mr. _____ to be cooperative.

A: I did.

Q: He didn't hold any documents back from you; is that correct?

THE IRS: Objection, Your Honor. The witness has already testified that Mr. _____ was cooperative.

Q: I imagine that when you did the TCMP audit, you verified the income figures, bank deposits, and such?

A: I did.

Q: So you looked for excluded income; is that correct?

A: Right.
Q: You didn't find any?   A: No.

Q: Apparently other than the items that were raised in your audit, there was nothing else, like travel and entertainment, any abuse in those areas, is that correct?
A: There were small de minimis items, but nothing of any consequence.
Q: At the end of your audit, was Mr. _____ ready to discuss the charitable contribution issue with you?
A: Yes. He had no qualms about discussing it.
Q: And you found yourself that it was an interesting issue, did you not?   A: Oh, yes.
Q: And you were interested in various analogies that he went through in arriving at his figures regarding the contribution?
A: I was fully aware how Mr. _____ arrived at his $88,583 figure on his 1981 return, and what he did prior to that.
PETITIONER: That's all the questions I have, Your Honor.
THE COURT: Any redirect?
THE IRS: Nothing further, Your Honor.
THE COURT: Then you may call your next witness.

IRS WITNESS No. 2:   Manager

The IRS's next witness was Agent No. 2 (male) whom we designate as WITNESS (R2). He was duly sworn, and thereupon described his accounting and business background and his 15 years with the Internal Revenue Service. The IRS's attorney then began his step-by-step direct examination.

THE IRS: At the time of the years at issue herein, what was your position with the Internal Revenue Service?
WITNESS (R2): I was Group Manager of the Compliance Division in San Jose, California.
Q: Briefly describe for us the function of your compliance group?
A: Its function was to have a focal point to track abusive type returns, whether they be tax shelters or protester activity. At the time, we had a barrage of 1040 returns with abusive charitable contributions, primarily the Universal Life Church. We selected those returns where our experience had shown that the taxpayers would give us a hard time during the audit process.

THE COURT: And it was your intent, when you looked at these returns, to decide whether or not they were tax protester returns?
WITNESS (R2): Yes.
THE COURT: In your opinion?
WITNESS (R2): In my opinion, as protesters. The brunt of these returns were designated as Universal Life Church cases.

Q: Mr. _____, do you recall the audit of the Petitioners' income tax returns for 1981, '82, and '83? Was the audit done in the group which you supervise?
A: Yes, I do. And, yes, it was.
Q: Did you have any prior knowledge of the Petitioner, Mr. ____ before the audit?
A: Yes, I did.
Q: When was this?
A: One of my functions as a group manager was to track areas of noncompliance and be aware of the tax preparers in our District and the kinds of returns they prepared, and to be aware of preparers' own tax returns. In that process, I was aware of Mr. _____'s previous court proceedings in the District Court and his activity on his own returns at that time: 1972-76.

Q: Do you know why Mr. _____'s '81-'83 returns   were assigned to the compliance group?
A: They were designated as protester returns.
Q: Did you have occasion to speak with Mr. _____ concerning the audit outcome?
A: Yes, approximately November 5th 1984.
Q: And what was the gist of your conversation?

A: I indicated that the charitable deduction on his Schedule A was inappropriate for somebody in the tax preparation business. I told him that I didn't want to see the deduction again on subsequent returns. In that process, I asked him why he continued to take the position he did, regarding his self-employment Social Security tax.
     He indicated that he couldn't get the President of the United States or Congress to act on his idea of renouncing his lifetime Social Security benefits, so he decided to try it with his tax returns.
THE IRS: Nothing further.
THE COURT: You may cross-examine.

One Revealing Exhibit

The petitioner's attorney notified the court that his cross-examination of IRS Agent No. 2 would consist of having him verify just one exhibit. The court said: "Certainly. Just hand him a copy." Thereupon, the petitioner's attorney proffered WITNESS (R2) Exhibit 59-BG dated November 6, 1984.

PETITIONER (addressing the witness): Mr. _____, was this a letter that you received from my client, Mr. _____, after the conversation you just testified to?
WITNESS (R2):   Yes, it is.
PETITIONER: I have no other questions, Your Honor.

THE COURT: You have no other questions?
PETITIONER: No.
THE COURT: Let me read this before I excuse the witness, because I may want to ask some questions.
THE IRS: Your Honor, I have one question on redirect examination.
THE COURT: Okay. Fine. Go ahead.

THE IRS: Mr. _____, do you remember the date of your telephone conversation with the Petitioner?
A : November 5, 1984.
THE COURT: And this was written November 6th?
A : Yes.
THE COURT: Does this letter coincide with your recollection of approximately what happened on November 5th?
A :   I remember informing Mr. _____ that it was my position to assert the civil fraud penalty, but with regard to all those quotations, I don't recall the majority of that.
THE COURT: Well, what do you recall about the conversation?

Editorial Note: This question was asked the witness on March 15, 1989. Exhibit 59-BG (the "letter") was written on November 6, 1984. The testified telephone conversation took place on November 5, 1984 between the hours of 2:30 to 3:15 p.m. See Figure 9.2 for selected excerpts from the 2-page, single-spaced typewritten letter on petitioner's business letterhead.

PETITIONER'S BUSINESS LETTERHEAD

Mr. _____

Group Mngr. , Compliance Div.

IRS, San Jose, CA 95103

November 6, 1984

Re: Phone Conversation
November 5, 1984

Dear Mr. _____

You phoned me asking what my position was on the Social Security matter at issue for the years 1981, 1982, and 1983.

I responded saying that: "In May 1981, I made a good faith, one-time, unconditional public gift of my lifetime Social Security benefits. This gifting raises two issues: one, the proper valuation of the gift, and, two, whether continued self-employment contributions to Social Security would be required."

You stated that: "There was no gift. Your whole idea is outrageous, preposterous, and frivolous. So much so that we are going to recommend the 50% civil fraud penalty against you. And I'm going to warn you right now: If you claim a charitable deduction for this on your 1984 return, I guarantee you I'll turn this over to our Criminal Investigation Division and recommend the 100% criminal fraud penalty in addition to the 50% civil fraud penalty."

You then castigated me: "We're getting sick and tired of you tax preparers around here. This whole mess sounds too much like a tax protest. We have additional penalties that we can assess against tax protestors, as you know."

I responded: "Yes, I know. But I am exercising a fundamental right under Amendment 9."

You asked sharply: "What Amendment 9?"

I answered you: "Amendment 9 of the U.S. Constitution. I am reluctant to mention the word 'Constitution' to you, as I know how antagonistic the IRS is towards it. Unless specifically excluded by law or regulation, I do have an inherent right to make a public gift of my Social Security benefits if I want to."

You snapped back: "No you don't! You don't have any such rights!"

Yours Truly,

/s/

_____

Fig. 9.2 - Excerpts from Petitioner's EXHIBIT 59-BG

A: I remember spending significant time in the conversation telling Mr. _____ that my position was that as a practitioner he had a higher standard to follow. I wanted to get that point across, and that's why I was fairly adamant about the civil fraud penalty.

THE COURT: But basically, other than that, this exhibit is more or less what took place?

A: I would say yes.

THE COURT (addressing the attorneys): Anything further from either of you?

PETITIONER: Nothing, Your Honor. No rebuttal testimony.

THE IRS: Nothing further, Your Honor.

THE COURT: All right. That concludes this trial.

Continuing Into Trial II

Trial II focused on the petitioners' 1985 and 1986 tax returns. As the judge was preparing to hear testimony from the first witness — Petitioner (H) — the IRS's attorney interjected the following "request"—

THE IRS: Your Honor, one of the witnesses listed on the Respondent's trial memo, Revenue Agent _____, was involved in an automobile accident and is unavailable today to testify. I would request preliminarily that we be allowed to leave the record open to take his testimony, in the event that we choose to do so. We can substitute, however, Revenue Agent [Witness (R2)] who testified in the previous trial.

THE COURT: Well, I won't rule on that now. Let's see how this trial goes.

Thereupon, WITNESS (P1) was duly sworn and resumed his earlier testimony, this time focusing on the 1985-'86 returns, and the "gap year" 1984. The culled testimony follows—

PETITIONER: Prior to filing your 1985 return, were you under audit for the earlier years?

WITNESS (P1): Yes, I was.

Q: When did that audit start and end?

A: It started June 1984 and ended November 1984.

Q: At that point in time, did you and the Internal Revenue Service have a disagreement over the deduction of the charitable contribution?
A: We certainly did.

Q: Did anybody in the IRS tell you that they would be looking into your subsequent years' returns?
A: Yes. I was threatened with the 100% criminal fraud penalty if I tried to claim this on my 1984 return.
Q: Did you have any expectation that your 1985 and 1986 returns would be audited?
A: Yes, I did.
Q: Who audited you for 1985 and 1986?
A: Mr. _____, Revenue Agent, Group 2401.

Q: Did he give you an audit report?   A: Yes.
Q: Did that audit report propose a fraud penalty?
A: No.
Q: Did the 90-day letter (Notice of Deficiency) propose a fraud penalty?
A: No. It did not.
Q: Then how did the fraud penalty for 1985 and 1986 come about?
A: It came about at the insistence of Mr. _____, Manager of Compliance, when the IRS's Answer to my Petition was filed.

Universal Life Church: Again!

The IRS's attorney proceeded with his penetrating cross-examination of WITNESS (P1). He proceeded zealously with direct examination of IRS WITNESS (R1), the 1981 auditor, and IRS WITNESS (R2), the group manager. The entire line of questioning and exhibits refocused on petitioner (H)'s perjurious affiliation with the Universal Life Church during the period 1972-1976. There were approximately 100 pages of testimony on these matters. Finally, the Trial II judge jumped in and said (to the IRS)—

THE COURT: I'm telling you now, for the second or third time, that I will not receive any more testimony allegedly relating to supposed contributions to the Universal Life Church, and any claimed deductions therefor. That is completely outside the scope of this case.

THE IRS: Very well, Your Honor.

At this point, the petitioner's attorney was permitted to cross-examine WITNESS (R2), the IRS group manager. The culled testimony follows—

PETITIONER: Over the phone, did you tell Mr. _____ that if he took this charitable deduction in subsequent years, that you would refer him for criminal fraud?
WITNESS (R2):   I think I told him that, yes.
Q: Did you say that you knew of Mr. _____ prior to all of this?
A: Yes, I did.
Q: Were you tracking him personally?
A: No, I wasn't. I was tracking him as the compliance group manager, and also having responsibility for preparers, and Mr. ____ was known to me as a "questionable preparer."
Q: And that was because of his alleged association with the Universal Life Church in 1972-76?
A: Yes, plus trying to opt out of the Social Security system by his renunciatory actions.
Q: You didn't think that he had a right to test whether or not he might be exempt from the self-employment tax after renouncing all of his lifetime Social Security benefits forever?
A: The issues that he was raising and the claims he was making are, in my opinion, so far outside the law as to constitute protester-type activity, subject to penalties.
Q: Okay. And what do you think he's protesting?
A: He's protesting the Social Security system and he's using the tax return inappropriately, and I find that that crosses the line for me over to the area of fraud.

Trial II abruptly ended on this note.
In their subsequent written opinions, both TC judges (Trial I and Trial II) concluded that fraud was NOT present. Concurrently, they "redetermined" that the 50% fraud penalty which the IRS had assessed *separately* against the petitioner and his wife would not apply. However, both judges succumbed to the IRS's alternative 20% substantial understatement penalty on the husband's self-employment tax, re Schedules SE.

10

AT TRIAL: ISSUE IV

Issue IV Addresses The Deductibility Of Attorney Fees And Deficiency Interest As Business Expenses On Schedule C. The IRS Also Asserted A $94 Negligence Penalty. The Attorney Fees Were For (1) Appeal of Trial I Decision On Issue II, And (2) Representation At Trial II For RESURRECTED Issues II And III. The Deficiency Interest Was The Portion "Attributable" To Schedule C By PHANTOM Accounting Changes Re Issue II. Petitioner Appeared PRO SE (Without Attorney), Which Avoided Any Subsequent Dispute Over Attorney Fees.

The trial aspects of Issue IV are instructional in several respects. Foremost, they exemplify the dollar magnitude of the expenditures that can be incurred in real life Tax Court proceedings such as Trials I and II herein. The overall cost for these two prior trials came to $144,529 ($92,278 for attorney fees and $52,521 for deficiency interest). This total cost *excludes* the amount of tax "redetermined" and the automatic add-on of penalties for negligence and understatement.

Issue IV at trial also exemplifies the foot-dragging by the IRS and by the Tax Court on rather simple issues. The amounts claimed on the author's 1990 and 1991 returns ($28,145 for legal fees and $34,507 for deficiency interest) were not in dispute. They were fully substantiated well before the TC proceeding. It is *where* they were claimed that was disputed. The author claimed them as business expenses; the IRS asserted they were personal expenses.

Had the author been a corporation instead of a Schedule C proprietorship, the expenses would have been allowed as business. Yet, the time lapse between the IRS's 90-day letter and the final decision of the Tax Court spanned two years and six months [2-18-93 to 8-22-95].

For Issues I, II, and III, we intentionally put aside trial testimony on the lesser penalties of negligence and understatement. In Issue IV, the IRS asserted a $94 negligence penalty. We'll present testimony on this, to illustrate how the IRS "penalty smears" a petitioner in order to recharacterize $62,652 (28,145 + 34,507) in legal fees and deficiency interest as personal expenses rather than business.

Issue IV also illustrates the informality of TC trial procedures when a petitioner represents himself *pro se* (without an attorney). By the same token, the informality enables the IRS to distort applicable facts and law without being under oath. Issue IV is a classic example of how the IRS gets away with ignoring the legislative intent of Section 162 (trade or business expenses) and Section 163 (business interest on phantom deficiencies caused by fictitious accounting changes). Issue IV is another manifestation of the unlevel playing field when involved with the IRS.

Petition Filed Within 2 Days

The IRS audit of the author's 1990 and 1991 Schedule C returns were completed on December 11, 1992. After indicating his disagreement with the auditor, he author requested that a 90-day deficiency notice be issued immediately. Some 60 days later (on February 18, 1993), said notice was received. A petition to the Tax Court was filed on February 20, 1993 — just two days after the IRS's deficiency notice.

The petition consisted of 10 pages following the format of Figure 4.2. There were 17 assignments of errors and 25 statements of facts. The petition was prepared by the author himself to avoid further IRS dispute over attorney fees. As such, the petition was filed—

In Propria Persona (in proper person).

To give you a taste of the specificity cited in the petition, we present two selected assignments of errors from the total of 17.

As to attorney fees, the petition read—

*It is an error to disregard the regulatory provisions of Treas. Reg. 1.162-1(a) that legal fees and expenses are deductible when ". . . **directly connected with or pertaining to** the taxpayer's trade or business."* [Emphasis added.]

As to deficiency interest, the petition read—

*It is an error to disregard the regulatory provisions of Treas. Reg. 1.163-9T(b)(1)(i) which exempts from the definition of personal interest that which is ". . . **properly allocable** . . . **to the conduct of** a trade or business.* [Emphasis added.]

The emphasized phrases are lifted directly from Treasury Department regulations which both the IRS and the Tax Court are supposed to uphold. We emphasize "supposed to." As you'll see later, neither agency — the IRS nor the Tax Court — has to follow the law in all circumstances.

The IRS, of course, denied all of the petitioner's allegations. Subsequently, on November 26,1993, the petitioner received: NOTICE SETTING DATE FOR TRIAL. The trial date was set for February 18, 1994 [Docket No.: 3952-93].

Subpoena of IRS Agent

Once a date is set for trial, each party has the right to subpoena witnesses in its behalf (TC Rule 147). Official subpoena forms, issued under the seal of the Tax Court, are obtained from the Office of the Clerk, Washington, D.C. An abbreviated version of a TC subpoena form is presented in Figure 10.1. The key instruction thereon is—

YOU ARE HEREBY COMMANDED to appear before the United States Tax Court — — — — — — and not to depart without leave of the Court.

United States Tax Court
WASHINGTON, D.C. 20217

Petitioner,
v.

COMMISSIONER INTERNAL REVENUE,

Respondent

} Docket No. ------------------

SUBPOENA

To --

YOU ARE HEREBY COMMANDED to appear ------------------------------

At ----------(time)----------(date)----------(place)---------------------

Then and there to testify on behalf of --------------------------------

and to bring with you ---

----

and not to depart without leave of the Court.

Dated -------------------

/s/

Petitioner or Respondent

/s/

Clerk of the Court

DECLARATION OF SERVICE
- - - - by tendering fees and mileage to - - - -

Fig. 10.1 - Format of Subpoena Obtainable from Tax Court

As per TC Rule 174(c), service of a subpoena—

shall be made by delivering a copy thereof to such person named therein and by tendering to such person the fees for one day's service and the mileage allowed by law.

In other words, when serving a subpoena upon an IRS agent, you must accompany the subpoena with a check payable to the IRS for each day's witness fee (typically $40 per day) and for each mile of travel (typically 30¢ per mile).

The petitioner prepared the official subpoena forms for service upon the IRS agent, Group Manager, who had been "tracking" the petitioner as a tax preparer since 1972. This agent was the instigator of the fraud penalty in Issue III. The purpose of the subpoena was to have the agent testify as to the origin and character of the Issue IV legal expenses, with respect to the petitioner's business as a tax preparer.

Although TC Rule 147(c) says that a subpoena may be served by a U.S. Marshal, such marshal will *not* serve upon an IRS agent. A private process server must be engaged. Even then, a process server cannot serve directly upon an IRS agent in person. It must be served indirectly through the Special Procedures Office of the nearest IRS District headquarters. This was done and a *Declaration of Service* (lower portion of Figure 10.1) was properly executed by the process server.

The very next day, the Special Procedures Officer called the petitioner and wanted to know what testimony the designated IRS agent was to give. The petitioner was also informed that "special authorization" by the IRS District Director would be required before the subpoenaed agent could testify. Further, the petitioner was notified that the IRS would file a MOTION TO QUASH SUBPOENA on the grounds that the subpoena is—

Unreasonable and oppressive in demanding the testimony of Group Manager [IRS agent].

Unreasonable and oppressive? These are exact words lifted from a 5-page official IRS motion to quash the petitioner's subpoena.

Objection to IRS's Motion

At trial, a copy of the IRS's motion to quash subpoena was handed to the petitioner approximately 30 seconds before the T.C. judge entered the courtroom. Anticipating this sleight-of-hand maneuver, the petitioner prepared on OBJECTION to the anticipated IRS motion, and filed it with the Court some 20 days earlier.

The petitioner's objection motion comprised four pages. Select portions thereof, pertinent to our presentation here, are as follows:

1. *Respondent's agent, _____, instigated the civil fraud penalty against petitioner on the sole basis that petitioner was a "protester-type tax preparer" [Tr II, p. 166]. To do this, _____ overrode three other agents of the respondent who found no fraudulent activity [Tr II, pp. 44, 45, 182, 183]. _____ also overrode the District Director who issued two Notices of Deficiency which did not include the fraud penalty.*

2. *There has been an ongoing pattern of hostility between _____ and the petitioner since about 1976 [Tr II, p. 166]. . . . At one point, _____ threatened petitioner with criminal fraud [Tr II, p. 182] if petitioner took on a "test case" re Sec. 132(g) of P.L. 92-603, which _____ never researched [Tr II, p. 63]. The petitioner took _____ up on his threat; hence the fraud assertion.*

3. *The fraud assertion was based solely on a "high propensity" assumption by _____ that petitioner might do something wrong; that the petitioner (as a tax preparer) "absolutely" was a danger to the Internal Revenue Service [Tr II, pp. 187-189].*

(The abbreviation **Tr** is for Trial **T**ranscript.)

Before any proceedings began, the judge ruled:

The Court has received respondent's motion to quash subpoena, and has also received an objection to respondent's motion to quash subpoena from petitioner. After reviewing both documents, the Court will grant respondent's motion to quash subpoena [Tr III, p. 4; l 5-13].

THE IRS: Thank you, Your Honor

Apparently, the Court was submitted a copy of the IRS's Motion to Quash some time before the petitioner was handed a copy. It's interesting how quickly the Court ruled in favor of the IRS.

No IRS Witness

Granting the IRS's motion to quash petitioner's subpoena of an IRS agent meant that there would be no IRS witness to testify. This also meant that the IRS attorney representing the Commissioner would be able to make statements to the Court, and not be under oath as to correctness. The petitioner's testimony, however, would be under oath. Being the only witness, the petitioner's testimony at Trial III is designated in the transcript as, simply: THE WITNESS.

In a "Pro Se" trial, certain informalities are allowed. The petitioner is allowed to make his own statements and narration of events to the court. He is subject to interrogation first by the Court, then by the IRS attorney. Any statements by the IRS attorney are subject to interrogation only by the Court. However, the petitioner can make rebuttal statements to whatever answers, points, exhibits, and arguments the IRS makes to the court. Because of the informality allowed, testimony by the witness, interrogations by the Court, and statements by the IRS can become disjointed and defocused.

As a starting point to the issues involved, the following exchange took place—

THE COURT: Now, let me ask this question of both parties. There's no question about the amount of legal fees that are in issue, is that correct?

THE WITNESS: That's correct.

THE IRS: Your Honor, there are really no factual issues. There are no substantiation issues. The only issues are whether legal expenses incurred in --

THE COURT: But the amount of legal expenses is the amount that you jointly stipulated, I take it?

THE IRS: Yes, Your Honor.

THE COURT: And you stipulated the interest expense?

THE IRS: Yes, Your Honor.

THE COURT: So we have those numbers that we start from?
THE IRS: Yes, Your Honor
THE COURT: All right. Proceed, sir (addressing the witness).

Origin of Deficiency Interest

The witness explained that the interest paid in 1990 and 1991 was for deficiency assessments on Schedules A and Schedules C for tax years 1981, 1982, and 1983. He pointed out that the deficiencies on Schedules A were for disallowed charitable contribution deductions, and that those on Schedules C were for tax book development expenses under Section 174(a): Research and Experimental Expenditures. By means of Joint Exhibit 3-C, he explained the computation showing that the ratio of the Schedules C deficiency interest to the total deficiency interest for Schedules A **and** Schedules C came to 60.22% . . . exactly.

Relevant to the above, the following exchange took place—

THE WITNESS: With respect to the deficiency interest, I would like to approach this item first. . . . In 1981, I launched a rather major tax book development project, which was a six-year project. . . . So, on my Schedules C for 1981, 2, and 3, I listed my expenditures under Section 174(a). Now, the --
THE COURT: Let me ask you this, because it might be relevant. Did the prior Court find that there were business expenses, or not?
THE WITNESS: That was not the issue. The expenses were allowed, but had to be spread out over three years. I elected under Section 174(a) to currently expense them on Schedule C. The Court allowed them, but required under Rule 155 that they be spread out over three years rather than being currently deductible. So, they were allowed in full; there were no other issues on Schedule C for those years.
THE COURT: Well, if the Court allowed them, that would be business, would it not?
THE WITNESS: I would say so, yes.
THE IRS: The Court did not find that he was in the business of preparing tax books, Your Honor. The Court allowed

him to capitalize research and experimental expenditures, and the Court did note that he was a tax book author.

Phantom Deficiency Created

By "spreading out" over three years, the initially claimed Section 174(a) expenses on each sequential Schedule C ('81 through '86), a *phantom deficiency* was created for years '81 through '83. A good portion of the testimony was pointing out to the court, step by step, how the phantom deficiencies for the initial years actually created surplus deductions on the Schedules C for years '84 through '86. Petitioner used his Exhibit 13 to describe the accounting recharacterization that took place. A condensation of the Exhibit 13 is presented in Figure 10.2.

The actual testimony on the "phantom" deficiency aspects of Schedule C did not go as smoothly as the above digest suggests. Nevertheless, a sampling of the testimony is as follows—

THE WITNESS: Your Honor, I'd like to make a comment on an exhibit I'd like to introduce. It pertains to the tabulation of deficiency interest by the IRS, and how the Schedule C items . . . went through all the way from '81 to '86. . . . This points out that it was strictly an accounting change to the Schedules C. Prior courts have ruled that -- if there were no changes in income, other than through accounting changes, it was treated as ordinary expense in connection with that particular trade or business.

And that's the point I'm trying to make here today. . . . That this was strictly only an accounting change, and by doing so, it created phantom deficiency in 1981, 2, and 3, which made for this great amount of deficiency interest that we're talking about here, some $52,000 by the way. I'd like to offer this into evidence, Your Honor.

Exhibit 13 was admitted into evidence. There following another 12 pages of transcript testimony, rehashing the above and cross-checking year by year. At this point—

ISSUE II (Prototype Expenses) on Sch.C as "Sec. 174(a)"							
//// EXPENSE AMOUNTS INITIALLY CLAIMED ////							
YEAR	1981	1982	1983	1984	1985	1986	AMOUNT ALLOWED $
////	$47,868	$8,602	$51,841	$46,535	$13,712	$41,222	
1981	15,956						15,956
1982	15,956	2,867					18,823
1983	15,956	2,868	17,280				36,104
1984		2,867	17,281	15,512			35,660
1985			17,280	15,511	4,571		37,362
1986				15,512	4,570	13,741	33,823
1987					4,571	13,740	18,311
1988						13,741	13,741
Totals	47,868	8,602	51,841	46,535	13,712	41,222	209,780

Fig. 10.2 - "Phantom Changes" Caused by 3-year Prorations of Issue II

THE WITNESS: Now, so much for deficiency interest, unless there are other comments or questions that the Court may have, or that the IRS counsel may have. We'll get into legal expenses in a minute.

THE COURT: (Addressing the IRS attorney). Let's approach this issue by issue, which I think makes it clearer to all of us. Would you like to cross-examine the petitioner?

THE IRS: That's fine, Your Honor. Some of the questions I have will address both issues.

Penalty Regurgitations

The issue before the Court at this point was the phantom deficiency interest allocable to Schedule C, created by a prior Court-induced accounting change, which produced no real net income or expenses. The IRS attorney successfully distracted the Court's attention from this accounting issue by regurgitating old penalty issues addressed by the two prior Courts. The petitioner objected to this, but Judge III allowed it, because of petitioner's mentioning Issue II in those two prior cases. The petitioner was concerned about what portion of the $52,000 "plus" that was allocable to Schedule C as a business expenses: the IRS was more interested in "penalty smearing" the petitioner. After all, the IRS had asserted a $94 penalty as part of Issue IV. For this endeavor, the IRS questioning took up about 20 pages of transcript testimony. Samples of the IRS questions follow—

THE IRS: Mr. _____, another issue of Tax Court Trial I was whether you were liable for additions to tax by negligence; isn't that correct?

(From this question on, we'll use the Q and A format: "Q" for question by IRS; "A" for answer by the witness/petitioner.)

A: Yes.
Q: That Court determined that you were liable for negligence, isn't that correct?
A: Yes.
Q: Also, in Tax Court Trial I, you were found liable for a substantial underpayment penalty; isn't that correct?
A: Yes.
Q: Another issue was whether you were liable for fraud; isn't that correct?
A: Yes.
Q: The Court found that you were not liable for fraud, or, rather, the Court determined that the respondent had not met its burden; isn't that correct?
A: Yes.
Q: Again, there was the issue of negligence, correct, in Tax Court Trial II?
A: Yes.
Q: And again, there was the issue of substantial understatement of income tax; isn't that correct?
A: Yes.

Q: And again, there was the issue of fraud for Tax Court Trial II; isn't that correct?

A: Yes.

Q: For Tax Court Trial II, the Court found you to be negligent with regard to taking the social security benefits deduction, even though you had already conceded the issue. Isn't that correct?

A: There was no negligence penalty, and no penalties for Tax Court II. There was no deficiency, no penalties, no nothing.

THE COURT: Well, they were originally asserted by the respondent in the notice of deficiency for Tax Court II.

THE WITNESS: But the net effect, Your Honor, there were no penalties applied for Trial II.

THE COURT: No, but the Court would make a finding with regard to what was then asserted in the notice of deficiency.

THE WITNESS: Oh, I see. Okay.

THE COURT: Okay. It's obvious in both decisions the Court ruled against petitioner.

THE IRS: And finally, simply to be complete, the Court [in Trial II] determined again that the respondent had not met its burden of proof with regard to the addition to tax for fraud; isn't that correct?

THE WITNESS: That's correct.

The net effect of this whole line of IRS questioning was to bias TC Judge III with a rehash of penalty issues heard by the prior two TC judges. The only reference to deficiency interest was the IRS attorney's assertion that it was disallowed as a business expense because that was the official IRS position on the matter.

Next, Those Legal Fees

The IRS attorney next started asking questions about legal fees. The judge interrupted her by saying—

Why don't you let petitioner put on his position on legal fees, then you can cross-examine him.

As summarized in his pre-trial memorandum, the petitioner had paid a total of $28,145 in legal fees for 1990 and 1991. Of this amount, $20,484 was paid to Attorney A for representation at Trial II for '85 and '86; $7,661 was paid to Attorney B to appeal the decision in Trial I relative to the 3-year versus 1-year expensing of petitioner's tax book development effort in '81, '82, and '83. As to Trial II, the initial Notice of Deficiency alleged $432 in penalties. Before Trial II took place, the IRS's "irate agent" whom the petitioner had subpoenaed, amended the Notice of Deficiency to **add** $9,136 in fraud penalties. Selected examples of this testimony follow.

THE WITNESS: With respect to the legal fees, there were two attorneys involved, Mr. _____ [A] and Mr. _____
[B}; both were admitted to practice before the Tax Court. Mr. A's expenses were for representation at Trial II which took place in December 1989. There were two key issues. One was the tax book development expenses on Schedule C. The other was the fraud penalty, which the subpoenaed witness had testified previously he had been tracking me since --
THE IRS: Objection, Your Honor; hearsay.
THE COURT: Sustained.
THE WITNESS: All right. One of the witnesses at that trial had indicated that being a tax preparer, that I might encourage some of my clients to voluntarily gift to the government their social security benefits. The whole thrust of that fraud issue portion had to do with my being a tax preparer.
THE IRS: Objection, Your Honor. I'm trying to understand where the petitioner is going with this.
THE COURT: It's obvious that the Court found that respondent did not carry their burden of proof; so you won on that issue. We know that.
THE WITNESS: What I'm trying to point out here is that the fraud issue was raised primarily because I was a tax preparer, and I was trying to protect my professional reputation in that regard.
THE IRS: Objection, Your Honor; mischaracterize.
THE WITNESS: Well, that's my characterization of it.

THE COURT: Well, I would think that most taxpayers who are accused of fraud would make that characterization. But it doesn't carry much weight.

THE WITNESS: Okay. Anyhow -- what I'm trying to get at is that part of the legal expenses had to do with defending my character as a tax preparer. Part also had to do with my tax book development expenses on Schedule C.

THE COURT: On the issue of your research expenses, when did you start making money as an author?

THE WITNESS: 1990.

THE COURT: 1990?

THE WITNESS: That is correct, Your Honor. I had a publisher, sold 9,000 books that year, and that's indicated on my 1990 Schedule C.

THE COURT: All right, fine.

THE WITNESS: And the purpose of my making comments about the asserted fraud penalty was that no objective standard was used. Just because I was a tax preparer, they [the IRS] were going to throw all the penalties at me that they could.

THE IRS: Your Honor, I object to that characterization of the respondent and any of the respondent's procedures or motives.

THE COURT: Yes, but one could assume that if somebody comes across a tax return preparer, and they do something you [the IRS] do not think is proper, you might be a little harsher on that particular individual than on somebody else, because they know what they are doing.

THE WITNESS: That was exactly --. In summarizing, the legal fees paid to Mr. __ [attorney A] were for Trial II representation and the filing of briefs and so forth. Afterwards, I actually received no bill, no assessment from the respondent for those years ['85 and '86]. In fact, I got a refund for both years.

Now, the IRS Again

THE IRS: Mr. _____, you referred to a decision document for Trial II in which there is a line which states, to be assessed: "None." You paid your deficiencies ahead of time, isn't that correct?

THE WITNESS: I didn't pay the deficiency. I paid the tax ahead of time. I conceded the charitable deduction issue on Schedule A and paid that amount ahead of time, because I had already conceded it in Trial I.

THE IRS: So actually, it's not correct --

THE COURT: You're saying that you made a partial payment, then, is that correct?

THE WITNESS: No. I paid it on the Schedule A item only; that's correct.

THE COURT: So you made a partial payment.

THE WITNESS: Yeah, but I got a refund.

THE COURT: And there were other items --

THE WITNESS: May I point out something else to the Court? She hasn't brought it up. What happened in this three year spreading out of the Schedule C items in '81, '82, and '83, it created on overpayment for years '85 and '86. So, there was no need for me to have thought about prepaying any deficiencies, or anything else.

THE IRS: Your Honor, the petitioner stated that there was no deficiency found by the Court, and I'm only trying to make it clear that there was a deficiency and penalties, in spite of the fact that no amount was due.

THE WITNESS: To clarify that, Your Honor, on the Joint Exhibit 9-I, she's talking about the memorandum decision; I'm talking about the entry decision. (Pause)

THE COURT: Petitioner is correct; 9-I shows that the deficiency to be assessed is "None."

THE IRS: Mr. _____, you have been able to substantiate the amount of legal fees at issue; isn't that correct?

THE WITNESS: Yes.

THE IRS: But you've been unable to apportion the legal fees; isn't that correct?

THE WITNESS: That is correct. I cannot apportion it. But let me add my comment to that. The negligence and other penalties that you alleged were "addressed" were alternatives to the fraud penalty.

Had the fraud penalty been upheld, some of these penalties wouldn't have come into existence.

THE IRS: Objection, Your Honor.

THE COURT: That's by statute.

THE WITNESS: Correct. My point is that the legal fees for 1990 and 1991 were primarily associated with Section 174(a) on Schedule C. That was the big money item. By '85 and '86, the Schedule A was a very minor money item. The alternate penalties were not even really addressed in Trial II.

THE COURT: Does the respondent agree that if the legal fees are not business related, they would otherwise be deductible on Schedule A?

THE IRS: Yes, Your Honor.

THE COURT: As I view it, we have a novel issue before us. I take it you're both finished now?

THE WITNESS: Yes, Your Honor.

THE IRS: I would like a minute or two to prepare for a closing statement, Your Honor, if that's fine with the Court.

THE COURT: No. This case stands submitted.

THE CLERK: All rise.

Whereupon the hearing was adjourned.

11

POST-TRIAL MATTERS

Following Trial, There Are Filings Of Briefs —
OPENING And REPLY; Findings Of Fact;
Memoranda Of Decisions; Rule 155
Recomputations; And Entry Of Decisions. The
Briefs Set Forth The "Legal Points" (Evidence,
Law, And Arguments) On Which Each Party
Relies. Each Trial Judge Extracts From The
Briefs That Which Is In Concert With His/Her
Views, To Form "Conclusions" Re Applicable
Deficiencies, Overpayments, And Penalties.
If Both Parties Agree On The RECOMPU-
TATIONS, And No Notice Of Appeal Is Filed,
The ENTRY OF DECISION Becomes Final.

Trial ends when the presiding judge excuses the last witness, or receives into evidence the last admissible document. This does not mean that every person present gets up immediately and walks out of the courtroom. There are certain post-trial matters to attend to. One of these matters is the clarifying of the markings of the admissible documents so that all parties are using the same identifying symbols. Then there are instructions for the filing of written briefs. A "brief" is a synopsis of the trial evidence, how said evidence relates to the applicable tax law (or laws), and what finding each party wishes the judge to make. A brief is a form of legal argument trying to convince the judge as to which party shall prevail . . . on each issue.

Approximately eight to twelve months after all briefs are in, a written report and decision by the court is forthcoming. There is no statutory requirement setting a specific time. The nearest requirement is Section 7459(a) of the IR Code which merely says—

A report upon any proceeding instituted before the Tax Court and a decision thereon shall be made as quickly as practicable.

Most TC judges are not interested in making bold decisions, nor in parting too radically from IRS positions. They don't want to be accused by the IRS of depriving government of its always much-needed revenue. So, they take their time and try to favor the IRS as much as possible.

Issue I (Public Gift) was conceded by the petitioner. Issue III (Fraud Penalty) was not proven by the IRS (as evidenced by testimony at Trial III). This leaves Issues II and IV for post-trial commentary. Consequently, in this chapter we want to familiarize you with the procedure on briefs, and tell you what the final decisions were. Where appropriate, we'll indicate the judicial rationale.

Time for Filing Briefs

TC Rule 151(a): Briefs, says—

Briefs shall be filed after trial or submission of a case, except as otherwise directed by the presiding Judge.

Subrules (b), (c), (d), and (e) specify the time for filing, service required, number of copies, and the form and content of briefs.

Opposing briefs may be filed simultaneously or seriatim (one after the other). Most TC judges prefer that the briefs be filed simultaneously. This permits the judge to review each party's arguments side-by-side. This way, he can be convinced or not convinced, or make the decision based on his own research.

For simultaneous briefs, there are two classifications: *opening* briefs and *reply* briefs. The term "opening" brief tends to be misleading. It is not prepared at the beginning of trial; it is prepared **after conclusion** of trial. It is the "opening" in the sense that it is the opening barrage of legal arguments that each side advances to support its cause.

Following each opening set of arguments, there are reply briefs. That is, each side is "replying" to the opening arguments of the other. Thus, it is self-evident that each trial requires four briefs: two opening briefs and two reply briefs. The opening briefs are filed simultaneously on one date. The reply briefs are filed simultaneously on another — later — date.

The dates for filing the briefs are set by each presiding judge. One factor that he considers before fixing the date is the time required for preparation of the stenographic transcript of the trial proceedings. Each party must have an official transcript in order to extract and reference the evidentiary matters that are important to its position. This usually takes about 30 days after conclusion of trial. It is for this reason that the opening briefs are judicially set at 60 to 90 days after the trial transcript is available. The reply briefs are then due between 30 and 60 days after the date on which the opening briefs are due to be filed. [TC Rule 151(b)(1).]

A schematic arrangement of the filing of briefs is presented in Figure 10.1. The arrangement is to help you keep in mind the immediate post-trial sequence of events.

Contents of Briefs

Contentwise, there is an extensive sequence of items that must be included, whether it be the opening brief or the reply brief. This sequence is as follows:

1. Table of contents with page references;
2. List of all cited cases arranged alphabetically stating the page of the brief on which each case is cited. Citations shall be in italics when printed and underscored when typewritten;
3. Statement of the nature of the controversy and of the amount of tax and penalty involved;
4. Statement of the issues to be decided;
5. Numbered statements of proposed findings of fact, based on the evidence at trial;

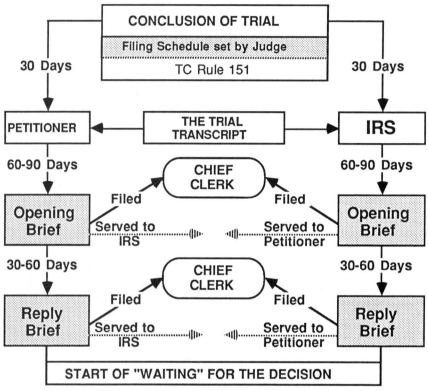

Fig. 11.1 - Time Sequence for Briefs Following Trial

6. Statement of the points of fact on which each party relies; and
7. Argument which sets forth and discusses the points of law involved and any disputed questions of fact.

As to the proposed findings of fact (item 5 above), each proposed finding must be complete and self-explanatory. It must be a concise statement of one essential fact at a time, and not be a recital of the testimony nor a discussion of the evidence or applicable law. Each numbered statement must contain references to the pages of the transcript or the exhibits or other sources relied upon to support the statement. The typical symbols used are **Tr** for transcript and

Ex for exhibit. For example, **Tr** 214:3-19 means: transcript, page 214, lines 3 to 19.

Those proposed findings of fact which are accepted by the judge become the basis for his/her decision. The judge is also influenced by those citations from other trials where the facts and circumstances may be similar to those under current consideration.

Issue II: Petitioner's Position

In his Trial I and Trial II briefs, petitioner subheaded his position on Issue II as EXPERIMENTAL EXPENDITURES. This term is that which is directly used in IR Code Sec. 174(a): Treatment as Expenses.

Under his "Proposed Findings of Facts," petitioner listed the following points, among others:

1. The expenditures were ordinary and necessary experimentation for demonstrating the authorship and production feasibility of an all-new 25-volume tax book series with innovative concepts.
2. The end developmental goal was a computer diskette in **complete prepress book form** (except for covers) for each separate tax book subject.
3. There was no way in the world to develop petitioner's end product without going through the agonizing phases "the old-fashioned way" of typesetting, galley proofs, graphic arts, page pasteups, book design, prepress proofs, and printing hard-copy samples for demonstration purposes.
4. The unsuccessful financial backing from commercial publishers was due largely to the fact that production savings in time, money, and errors by desktop computerizing had not been sufficiently demonstrated, and that the market niche for a new tax book series had not yet been established.
5. All unused demonstration samples in Phases I, II, and III were destroyed sequentially.

The petitioner then cited excerpts from the following Tax Court cases addressing Sec. 174(a):

Mayrath, 41 T.C. 582, 590: . . . *applies to development of "concept" of model or project*

Magee, T.C. Memo 1973-2, 32 TCM 1277, 1279 . . . *experimental activity shows little, if any, return during developmental stages*

Kilroy, T.C. Memo 1980-489, 41 TCM 292, 295 . . . *deduction allowed even when experimental expenditures produce a substantial loss*

Louw, 30 TCM 421; 71-326 P-H Memo TC, 1494 . . . *the expectation of producing the end product is not a statutory requirement where purpose is to "sell, lease, or license . . . to others . . . so that they may produce"* [the end product]

The petitioner continued with his citations by excerpting from a U.S. Supreme Court ruling in *Snow v. IRS*, 416 U.S. 500-504. In that landmark decision, the high court overturned prior disallowances by the Tax Court and the Appeals Court which had supported the various IRS positions.

In quite succinct terms, the high court expressly held that:

*It was an error to disallow the deduction, which was "in connection with" petitioner's trade or business, and the disallowance was contrary to the broad legislative objective of Congress when it enacted Sec. 174 to provide an **economic incentive**, especially for small and growing businesses, to engage in the search for **new products** and new inventions.* [Emphasis added.]

Issue II: IRS's Position

The IRS's position on Issue II was that the expenditures incurred were not experimental in the "laboratory sense" in that they did not pertain to the development of a "new invention." Furthermore, there was "no connection" between petitioner's Schedule C business as a tax preparer and the preparation of demonstration samples of a new line of tax books. Therefore, the expenditures must be capitalized rather than expensed.

The IRS supported its thesis with the following argument (excerpted from its Trial I brief commencing on page 45):

Books have been published for over five hundred years. The petitioner's tax books are not different from other published works. The claimed research and developmental expenditures consist of normal publication costs resulting in a printed book plus costs related to supplies for promotional activities. As a result, the petitioner's treatment of these costs as research and development expenses does not fall within the intent of Sec. 174(a) because they did not invent a new product or process. To the extent that the expenditures were for the production of demonstration samples for promoting a series of tax books, they are plainly not research and development expenses.

The IRS continued its line of argument above in its Trial II brief (commencing on page 29) as follows:

The petitioner lacks the requisite profit motive for his authorship of tax books. The vast majority of the claimed expenditures were for formulating the page layout, design and other publishing activities which resulted in a printed book. He printed the books knowing they were obsolete. He was not in the trade or business of being an author of tax books, as he never held himself out as such. Additionally, prospective publishers did not require the petitioner to have demonstration samples. The samples were not part of his tax practitioner business.

The IRS concluded its position argument with an appeal to the court that—

Should the Court find that the petitioner was engaged in the trade or business of being an author of tax books, the claimed research and development expenses should be capitalized under IR Code Sec. 263.

Petitioner's Reply: Issue II

In his two reply briefs (Trial I and Trial II), the petitioner tried to indicate to the court that Sec. 263 was clearly off point. This was self-evident by any ordinary reading of the statutory language. Section 263(a): General Rule, reads as—

No deduction shall be allowed for—
(1) Any amount paid out for new buildings or for permanent improvements or betterments made to increase the value of any property or estate. This paragraph shall not apply to— [seven exceptions].

One of the seven exceptions was research and experimental expenditures deductible under section 174. [Sec. 263(a)(1)(B).]

To counter the IRS's thesis that tax books were like other literary works, the petitioner replied—

The demonstration samples (prototypes) dealt with tax law, tax forms, tax administration, and taxpayer compliance. Tax law is technical, complicated, and controversial. It is constantly changing. It lacks totally the universal and pleasing attributes of literacy and historical works. The term "literary" relates to the formal, balanced, and polished language of literature in prose or verse. The position taken by the IRS that tax law and its controversy is "literature" is absurd.

The petitioner continued in his reply argument that—

For some inexplicable reason, the IRS has a long history of trying to defeat the legislative intent of IRC Section 174(a)(1). This legislation dates back to 1954 and has remained virtually unchanged since that time.

The very latest case on point is that of <u>Driggs v. U.S.</u>, 706 F. Supp. 20 (N.D. Tex. 1989). . . . The Court finds the intent of Congress regarding the deduction of research or experimental expenses to be plainly discernible from the language of Sec.

174(a)(1) itself. Absent a clearly expressed legislative intention to the contrary, the language of the statute itself must ordinarily be regarded as conclusive. The statute's plain language has been interpreted to mean that all costs incident to the development of an experimental or pilot model are classed as research or experimental expenditures. [Emphasis added.]

Written Decisions Required

All written decisions become a permanent record of the Tax Court. That is, when "entered" in the court records, they can be quoted as judicial precedents for similar cases in the future. This is not so for oral decisions from the bench (as for Issue I, for example). Thus, for precedent purposes, certain statutory requirements must be met.

Basically, there are only two requirements. The decision on each trial must include (1) FINDINGS OF FACT, and (2) *either* OPINIONS or MEMORANDUM OPINIONS. This is made clear in the first two sentences of Section 7459(b), to wit—

It shall be the duty of the Tax Court . . . to include in its report upon any proceeding its findings of fact or opinion or memorandum opinion. The Tax Court shall report in writing all its findings of fact, opinions, and memorandum opinions. [Emphasis added.]

There is a distinction between memorandum opinions and (outright) opinions. A memorandum opinion involves interactive issues where the decision on one issue affects the computational aspects of other issues or other items on a return which may not be at issue. In these situations, the court alone cannot redetermine the tax deficiency with certainty. It requires a "reworking of the numbers" by the parties involved. Hence, a memorandum decision allows time to recompute the deficiencies and penalties, before final entry is made in official records. Complicated issues and complicated cases usually involve memorandum decisions.

A straight opinion, on the other hand, is prepared where the correct deficiency, if any, can be redetermined solely from information in possession of the court. This usually involves single-issue or simple-issue cases, where no fraud or alternative penalties are asserted.

All written decisions include a restatement of the deficiencies and penalties asserted by the IRS in its Notice(s) of Deficiency. This is why, when a taxpayer prepares his Petition to the Tax Court, he must attach copies of these official notices. The court uses this information as its reference base for its redetermination efforts. This restatement is displayed at the beginning of the decision document and should not be confused with the decision itself. The decision must be read in full and recomputations, if any, must be made before the correct deficiency and correct penalty are known.

The decision is not prepared in accordance with any particular format. The findings and opinions are typed on plain paper, double spaced, with footnoted citations. The cover page is for court indexing and citation reference purposes. It, too, is typed on plain paper and appears as—

T.C. Memo_____
United States Tax Court

_____, Petitioner(s)
v. Commissioner IRS, Respondent

Docket No._____   Date Filed_____

_____[attorney[___, for petitioner(s)
_____[attorney]___, for respondent

Date Served_____

The Issue II Decision(s)

The Trial I court gives the rationale for its opinion on Issue II on pages 27-35 of its Memorandum Opinion. The court cited verbatim the statutory wording of Tax Code Section 174(a) [Experimental expenditures deductible as a current expense and not capitalized]. It then concluded that—

[There are] *two prerequisites for the current deduction of expenditures under section 174. First, the expenditures must be paid or incurred by the taxpayer . . . "in connection with his trade or business." Second, the expenses must be "research and experimental expenditures."*

With these two prerequisites in mind, the court then goes on to weigh the written arguments (the post-trial briefs) of the petitioner and the IRS. It addressed first the "in connection with" aspects of Section 174(a). In excerpted form, the court stated—

It is difficult to tell whether petitioner contends that he was in the business of being an author, since his primary argument is that the expenses he deducted were experimental expenditures in connection with his return preparation business. We consider the evidence here to be clear that the deductions . . . were not . . . experimental expenses of his return preparation business. He did not plan to use the guides in [said] business, but rather to sell them to any persons that he could.

[However], several factors indicate that petitioner was in the trade or business of being an author. He was definitely in the business of being a tax return preparer and thus should have had some knowledge of the subject matter of his guides. He expended a substantial amount of time and effort on each of the five [prototype] guides which he completed. He spent the sums set forth in our findings . . . for such expenses as editing, graphics, design, and printing. [And] he contacted numerous publishers in an attempt to find . . . financial backing for the mass marketing of his books. All these actions indicate that the petitioner expected that his efforts would result in the successful and profitable exploitation of his works.

The court then addressed the second prerequisite of Section 174, namely, that the expenditures be "research and experimental" in nature. On this item, the court said (again in excerpted form)—

Under section 1.174-2(a)(1), Income Tax Regulations, it is clear that, in order to be deductible under section 174, the *amounts expended must "represent research and development costs in the **experimental or laboratory sense.**" While, in a sense, the amounts in question were paid by petitioner to develop a new version of an existing product, . . . we conclude they were not research and development costs in the experimental or laboratory sense. Books, and the technology required to produce them, have been in existence for centuries. Petitioner did not improve on such technology, he merely produced a different type of book.*

The capstone to the court's opinion was set forth in its closing paragraph relating to Issue II. The court held that—

Respondent has determined that the amount expended in connection with preparing each tax guide for publication must be capitalized under section 263 and deducted over the useful life of that guide. We conclude that the petitioner has failed to show error in this determination.

The Issue IV Decision(s)

In Trial III, the court rendered its decision as to the Schedule C interest expense deduction this way:

Petitioner's claimed deduction was based on a formula that allocated the interest between his trade or business and personal nondeductible interest. However, petitioner failed to produce sufficient evidence to establish that the amounts used in his formula are correct. Accordingly, we sustain the respondent on this issue.

As to the deductibility of legal expenses on Schedule C, the court ruled that—

At trial, petitioner admitted that he could not apportion the legal fees between the business and nonbusiness tax controversies "in a mathematical way." Based on this, we find that the petitioner did not prove that legal fees were deductible as business expenses under section 162. In view of section 212(3), we find that these legal expenses are deductible [on Schedule A], *subject to the 2-percent floor under section 67(a) for miscellaneous itemized deductions.*

> *Editorial Note*: The above ruling is a classic example of the Tax Court bending over backwards on relatively simple issues to favor the IRS when it can. As to the interest expense decision, the court totally ignored the IRS's stipulation that there are "no substantiation issues": meaning that the amounts used in the formula were correct. As to the legal expenses, the duty of the court is to make some reasonable allocation where it is self-evident that business matters were involved. When given the opportunity, the Tax Court will always take the "easy way" out, thus favoring the IRS.

Now, TC Rule 155

The Memorandum decisions of Trials I and II both ended with the emphasized statement—

An appropriate Order will be issued and Decision will be entered under Rule 155.

(As to Trial III, entry under Rule 155 was not court direced, but the parties agreed to it anyhow.)

This raises the question: What is Rule 155?

Answer: It is a recomputational rule before entry of decision. It is particularly applicable where the decision on one issue, such as Issue II, alters the computational aspects of deficiencies, overpayments, and penalties on other issues.

By the time this point in the trial proceedings have been reached, both parties try to agree as best they can. But, in reality, Rule 155 is another pressure on the petitioner to concede on the minor issues of disagreement, just to get the case "over with." Dragging a 1981 matter out until 1990 (the decision memos were dated June 1990 and December 1990, respectively) adds substantial costs to the deficiencies through compounding interest and attorney fees. Nevertheless, Rule 155 provides opportunity to clean up all loose-end computational matters before a decision becomes enforceably final.

In most cases, the parties try to clean up matters under Rule 155(a): Agreed Computations. This rule reads in principal part as follows:

Where the Court has filed or stated its opinion determining the issues in a case, it may withhold entry of its decision for the purpose of permitting the parties to submit computations pursuant to the Court's determination of the issues, showing the correct amount of the deficiency, liability, or overpayment to be entered as the decision. If the parties are in agreement . . . they, or either of them, shall file promptly with the Court an original and two copies of a computation showing the amount of the deficiency, liability, or overpayment and that there is no disagreement that the figures shown are in accordance with the findings and conclusions of the Court. In the case of an overpayment, the computation shall also include the amount and date of each payment made by the petitioner. The Court will then enter its decision.

If the parties cannot agree, each submits its own computations separately to the court. Either party may then request the court to hear its arguments supporting its interpretation of the court's findings and conclusions. Said arguments, however, must be limited to computational aspects, and not be used to raise new issues or to introduce new evidence for decision.

Putting It All Together

The recomputation for Issue III was ZERO for all years at issue. No fraud penalty applied to any of the years 1981-1986. This was the only clear-cut decision in both trials. In other words, the IRS **did not prove** any of its 134 allegations of fraud (in its Answers and Briefs)!

The specific Entry Orders of Decision on Issue III were—

Trial I: *There is no addition to tax due from petitioners pursuant to IRC Sec. 6653(b) for the taxable years ending 1981, 1982, and 1983.*

Trial II: *There is no addition to tax due from the petitioners for the taxable years 1985 and 1986 pursuant to IRC Sec. 6653(b)(1)(A) and Sec. 6653(b)(1)(B).*

As to all other issues, namely: I, II, IV, and alternative penalties, the IRS made out quite well. The bulk of the alternative penalties and statutory interest derived from the phantom accounting changes to Issue II in Trial I. For that trial, the Rule 155 recomputations required 21 pages of documentation; for Trial II, 19 pages were required; and for Trial III, 12 pages were required. The overall results of these 52 pages of recomputations are presented in Figure 11.2.

Particularly note the huge bonus called: **statutory interest** (Sec. 6601), that the IRS got. The amount was a whopping $54,054! Said interest is compounded daily, and is imposed on the additional tax *plus* penalties, **from the initial due date** of each at-issue year return. When a dispute drags on for eight to 10 years, the statutory interest can substantially exceed the court-awarded deficiency and penalties.

In its drive to overwhelm and subdue the petitioner, the IRS conducted **seven audits**! The net tax increase (deficiencies less overpayments) came to $11,953 (31,760 − 19,807). Since the IRS lost on the fraud penalties, the court awarded it alternative penalties which totaled $12,118 (7,845 + 4,273). Recheck these amounts in Figure 11.2. The Tax Court, it seems, always wants to favor the IRS with alternative penalties. It's the "brother" syndrome.

In the case of overpayments (where a petitioner is due a refund), the IRS has to pay interest to the petitioner. This was the case for years 1985-1988 in Figure 11.2. But note how drastically much lower this interest is ($5,805) compared with that paid to the IRS ($54,054).

The end product of the recomputational effort under Rule 155(a) is a document entitled: COMPUTATIONS FOR ENTRY OF DECISION. Both parties sign this document and submit it to the court, together with a proposed DECISION ORDER for each trial judge to sign. Said Orders were signed respectively on—

☐ September 28, 1990 for Trial I

For Text Example Issues I, II, and IV						
YEAR	Recomputations		Alternative Penalties		Statutory Interest	
	Deficiency	Overp'mnt	(1)	(2)	To IRS	By IRS
	$	<$>	$	$	$	<$>
1981	18,078		3,378		31,846	
1982	5,003		2,461	2,825	15,051	
1983	2,287		1,912	1,448	5,624	
1984	★					
1985		<5,676>				<2,235>
1986		<4,198>				<918>
1987	★	<6,085>				<1,664>
1988	★	<3,848>				<988>
1989	★					
1990	3,453				1,493	
1991	2,839		94		855	
Totals	31,760	<19,807>	7,845	4,273	54,869	<5,805>
	★ Years NOT at issue; (1) Negligence; (2) Understatement					
	< > indicates payments or credits TO petitioner					

Fig. 11.2 - Recomputation of Disputive Amounts - Rule 155 Entry

☐ February 22, 1991 for Trial II

☐ August 22, 1995 for Trial III

Each judge's signature thereto constitutes *Entry of Decision* and, end of case.

12

SUMMARY & CRITIQUE

The Tax Court System Is Not Yet A "Level
Playing Field" Between Petitioner And IRS.
Improvements Are Needed Via Changes In The
Tax Code. More Explicit Deficiency Notices
Are Required; The IRS Should Be Allowed Only
One Presumption Of Correctness; And A
"Reasonable Nexus" Standard Should Apply To
Petitioner Positions. Disallowed Penalties
Should Be Reversed Against The IRS; Section
6663(b) On Fraud Should Be Repealed And
Replaced With OBJECTIVE CRITERIA; And
Inequities In Statutory Interest Should Be
Corrected. Ultimately, Taxpayers Deserve A
Better System Of Tax Justice Than Present
Tax Court Procedures Provide.

Like all processes in life, there are advantages and disadvantages
to Tax Court proceedings. The advantages lie primarily in the
structural concepts, the focused specialization, and the rules of
practice which attempt to equalize the adversarial rights between the
petitioner and the IRS.

The disadvantages lie primarily in the fact that the IRS is the sole
respondent, case after case. This enables it to develop techniques
and practices which raise ethics questions, but which slip through
the many loopholes in the Tax Court rules. Discovering,
expanding, and taking advantage of these loopholes — for no direct
cost out of its pocket — is only available to the IRS. This benefit
results from its repetitive experiences with the approximately 30,000
Tax Court cases that it handles each year.

Perhaps the greatest single disadvantage of the Tax Court system is that it cannot discipline the IRS in any way. It can discipline the petitioner with additional penalties beyond those that the IRS might impose. And it can dismiss a petitioner's case for lack of cause. It can never dismiss the IRS's case for lack of cause, because it (the Tax Court) is duty bound to "protect the revenue of government."

Nevertheless, where there is a substantial amount of tax plus penalty in dispute, Tax Court proceedings are the only game in town. Although tax disputes may be litigated in federal district courts, the reality is that these courts are not set up to handle in depth those issues requiring multiply-applicable tax laws. The Internal Revenue Code is a special monstrosity of its own.

Being the "only game in town" does not mean that the Tax Court system is devoid of all criticism. It is far from perfect. The Tax Court and the IR Code have a long way to go to curtail the many IRS abuses of power, privilege, and discretion. Consequently, in this chapter we are going to criticize the Tax Court system — constructively, we hope — so as to improve it and encourage other taxpayers to use it prudently when disagreeing with the IRS.

TC Rule 1(b) Misleading

Back in Chapter 1, we cited TC Rule 1(b). It is instructive for summary purposes to cite it again. It reads (in full)—

*These Rules shall be construed to secure the **just**, **speedy**, and **inexpensive** determination of every case.* [Emphasis added.]

We're sorry, but we think this statement is grossly misleading.

Let's take the three emphasized adjectives and apply them to the results of the At-Trial issues which we recapitulated for you in Figure 11.2. For reminder purposes, there were seven IRS audits involved! Basically, there were two underlying issues, namely: (1) a new idea on public gifting, and (2) experimental expenditures on a tax-book-development project. What happened as a result of the Tax Court process?

Is it a *just* system that permits the IRS to reap $54,054 in statutory interest for a net tax deficiency of $11,953 (31,760 − 19,807)? Is it a just system that permits the IRS to reap $12,118 (7,845 + 4,273) in alternative penalties because the IRS could not prove its 134 allegations of fraud? Or, is the Tax Court a punitive system that upholds the adversarial views of the IRS when it classifies a petitioner as a "tax protester," when the term does not appear in the Internal Revenue Code whatsoever?

Is it a *speedy* system when it takes 14 years (1981-1995) to settle the two underlying issues? Yes, there were peripheral issues, such as phantom accounting changes, alternative penalties, attorney fees, and statutory interest that extended the time span.

Is it *inexpensive* when it costs a petitioner $92,278 in attorney fees to defend against the IRS's false allegations of fraud, **and** simultaneously reward the IRS with some $50,000 (net) in statutory interest?

We know that no tax system is perfect. But how wide do we allow the imperfections to grow without, at some point, correcting the system?

We offer some corrective proposals in this regard. We are under no illusion that our proposals will ever be adopted. Nevertheless, the proposals made will provide you with a checklist of what to be aware of, should you become a petitioner in a Tax Court proceeding.

Must Shorten the Time

The cornerstone example that we used in prior chapters was a 1981 return. That particular return was filed with the IRS on January 27, 1982. The entry of decision on its disputive issues was made by the Tax Court on September 28, 1990. That's eight years and eight months to resolve a tax dispute. That's entirely too long. Even criminals get speedier justice than this.

Our contention is that the absolute maximum time to resolve any tax dispute should be statutorily set at six years. That's six years from *date of filing* a return to *date of entry* of decision thereon. This gives the IRS and the Tax Court adequate time to get their acts together. If entry of decision is not made on or before the statutory six years, the matter becomes automatically resolved in favor of the taxpayer/petitioner.

To accomplish the 6-year limitation period, modest amendments to the Internal Revenue Code are required. For example, Code Section 7459: Reports and Decisions (of the Tax Court), requires only one amending sentence. Said sentence could be—

In no event, however, shall a decision be entered after 6 years from the date of filing the return in dispute.

This sentence could follow subsection 7459(a) in which the clause "as quickly as practicable" appears.

Suspend Statutory Interest

There is a quick and easy way to shorten Tax Court proceedings and the IRS's foot-dragging. Simply suspend the running of statutory interest the moment a petition is docketed by the Tax Court. As we saw in Figure 11.1, the IRS got $54,054 in statutory interest. No wonder TC procedures drag out so. The amount of interest was *more than double* the net deficiency and alternative penalties. This is an inexcusable — and disreputable — way to generate revenue for government. Particularly so, when all tax returns and TC petitions were timely filed.

There is a smidgen of suspension relief already in the IR Code, but it doesn't apply in TC cases. Section 6601(c): Suspension of Interest in Certain Cases, applies only to waivers of assessment and collection procedures by the IRS. The existing unnumbered paragraph could be numbered (1), following by the addition of a paragraph (2), namely:

Where a petition has been timely filed with the Tax Court, the date of docketing shall be the date from which all statutory interest is suspended. It shall remain suspended until final entry of decision is made.

Furthermore, the rate of deficiency interest paid by taxpayers to the IRS should be identical to that rate paid by the IRS to taxpayers for overpayments. As things now stand, the IRS gets a 1% differential in its favor. There is entirely too much Big Brother favoritism in our tax laws. No wonder many taxpayers are cynical towards government and Congress.

Improve Deficiency Notices

This is supposed to be a nation of justice, fairness, and democracy. And yet, Congress and the President have let the IRS get away with its stereotyped and intimidating notices of tax deficiency. These notices must be made more specific and more explicit. Code Section 6212: Notice of Deficiency, could be amended by adding a new subsection (e): Contents of Notice.

Among the changes needed, each notice should include:

1. Date IRS audit completed.
2. Amount of IRS time spent on the audit and on the notice (helps petitioners gauge importance of issues).
3. Last date for petition to be filed.
4. Tax Court Petition Form 1
5. TC Information Sheet (reproduced from inside cover of TC Rules).

For each item of deficiency asserted, the notice should contain a clear and explicit attachment, such as—

(a) Findings of fact which form the basis of the IRS's "determination."
(b) Statement of the law or regulation (by section and subsection) on which the IRS relies for its position.
(c) List of citations (if any) of prior TC cases addressing the exact, or near exact, issue the IRS is raising.

We can hear the IRS protesting now—

"You mean that we have to disclose our legal position to the taxpayer before he goes into Tax Court? That's not fair. We have 'rights,' you know. We are the IRS!"

The problem is: the IRS is lazy, sloppy, and arrogant. It has too much power. Instead of relying on the intimidation of bureaucratic notices, it should act more responsibly towards taxpayers (who pay their salaries, vacations, and pensions).

We think the Tax Court itself should get behind the move for more specificity in the Notices of Deficiency. After all, these do become a mandatory attachment to every petition. More explicitness in the notices could save Tax Court time, taxpayer expense, and overall tax administration costs.

Impose "Reverse Penalties"

The standard practice on Notices of Deficiency is to display prominently the penalties that are asserted. The idea is to call immediate attention to the penalties and thereby traumatize the taxpayer into cowering to IRS demands.

Altogether, there are approximately 55 different penalties that the IRS can assess against taxpayers. They are identified in Sections 6651 through 6724 of the IR Code. The IRS gloats over the fact that it can pyramid these penalties ad infinitum. There are **no constraints whatsoever** against the IRS in its drive for maximum penalty revenue. Except for fraud, the burden of proof is on the taxpayer to show that the penalties do not apply.

We think that the burden of proof on *all* penalties — not just fraud — should be on the IRS. But we know that Congress likes the idea of raising revenue "without raising taxes." Penalties are euphemistically called: *additions to tax* . . . but not "raising taxes."

Penalty pyramiding is a form of extortion and willful oppression under the color of law. It is a form of knowingly demanding greater sums than were intended by the underlying tax laws. Section 7214: Offenses by Officers and Employees of the IRS, imposes a fine of $10,000 and/or five years imprisonment for willful oppression. But the Tax Court, as we related earlier, will not recognize Section 7214 as part of its "redetermination" jurisdiction.

Therefore, we propose an entirely new section of the tax code which is self-enforcing. We propose Section 6751: REVERSIBLE PENALTIES. The wording for such a section might read as—

Where the IRS has asserted any penalty in its Notice of Deficiency, other than for fraud, and such penalty is not sustained in the Entry of Decision of the Tax Court, that penalty — in the full amount assessed — shall be reversed against the IRS. The reversed amount shall be treated as an overpayment of tax and refunded promptly to the taxpayer/petitioner.

This is the only way to get the IRS to tone down its penalty mania against taxpayers. Surely, there must be some members in Congress who believe likewise.

Set Objective Criteria for Fraud

After nearly 85 years of federal income tax administration (1913 on), there are still no objective criteria defining fraud in the Internal Revenue Code. Nor are there criteria of any kind defining fraud in IRS/Treasury Regulations or in Tax Court rules. For such a serious penalty allegation, ordinary reasoning suggests that there should be some official definitive standard, guidelines, or checklist as to what constitutes fraud with intent to evade tax. The truth is: there is NO SUCH OBJECTIVITY!

Fraud, as asserted by the IRS, is based solely on the personal whim and vindictiveness of the revenue agent asserting it. In support of this accusation, recall the Issue III testimony on pp. 9-20 through 9-24. For a nation exalting its Judeo-Christian ethics, this IRS behavior is unacceptable.

Yet, the IRS recently inveigled Congress and the President to change the former 50% fraud penalty under former Section 6653(b) to 75%, and renumber it Section 6663 (effective after December 31, 1989). Does this new code section impose any objective standards on the IRS before it arbitrarily alleges fraud?

No. It does not. Would you believe that there is **n o** IRS/Treasury regulation accompanying Section 6663? Don't believe it? Have your own tax advisor confirm it to you, and compare with the voluminous regulations accompanying Section 6662 (alternative penalties).

Furthermore, the IRS crafted a new subsection 6663(b) which **shifts the burden of proof** from the IRS to the taxpayer. It sets a new standard for the taxpayer to disprove fraud "by a preponderance of evidence." This is a perversion of justice of the most reprehensible kind. Where were the Tax Court judges when the IRS slipped this one through?

Also, where was the (Congressional) Joint Committee on Taxation? This committee is duty bound by Sections 8022 and 8023 of the IR Code to investigate the IRS, and to call upon any other "instrumentality of government," such as the Tax Court, for recommendations for improving justice in the tax laws. The Tax Court, with its more than 65 years of adjudicating fraud cases, surely can come up with a credible checklist of **Indicia of Fraud** for embodiment in the tax code. There should be from six to nine statutory tests that the IRS must certify to, before it is authorized to allege fraud. These indicia tests must be signed by the responsible IRS official or agent . . . "under penalties of perjury."

Repeal/Replace Section 6663(b)

The new tax code subsection 6663(b) on fraud is applicable to all returns filed after 1989. This subsection now reads in full as—

If the [IRS] *establishes that any portion of an underpayment is attributable to fraud, the entire underpayment shall be treated as attributable to fraud, except with respect to any portion of the* underpayment **which the taxpayer establishes (by a preponderance of the evidence)** *is not attributable to fraud.* [Emphasis added.]

If this is not shifting the burden of proof to the taxpayer, we don't know what is.

Subsection 6663(b): Determination of Portion Attributable to Fraud, must be repealed outright. In its place, there should be a new subsection: MANDATORY CRITERIA BEFORE ALLEGING FRAUD. The above-mentioned Joint Committee should then prescribe the checklist indicia of fraud, in consensus with the Chief Judge of the Tax Court. The appropriate replacement wording might be—

> *Before the penalty prescribed by section 6663(a) can be alleged,*
> *the [IRS] shall furnish to the taxpayer a certified listing (under*
> *penalties of perjury) that one or more of the following indicia of*
> *fraud has/have been established, namely—*
> *(1) Understatement of income*
> *(2) Concealment of information*
> *(3) Inadequate records*
> [. . . and so on]

Then, in the event that fraud cannot be proven in Tax Court, a further subsection should be added. This would be subsection 6663(d): REVERSIBILITY OF FRAUD PENALTY. The wording of such a subsection might read—

> *Should the fraud penalty not be sustained in any trial or*
> *hearing, the IRS official or agent erroneously asserting it shall*
> *pay, from his personal earnings, to the taxpayer the same dollar*
> *amount as erroneously assessed. Such payment to the taxpayer*
> *shall be deemed a "personal injury liability assignment" which*
> *is excludable from the taxpayer's gross income under the*
> *provisions of Section 130.*

Subsection 6663(a): Imposition of Penalty, and subsection 6663(c): Special Rule for Joint Returns, would be unaffected by the above proposals. All we seek is that the IRS be made more responsible and accountable in its fraud allegations.

Allow Only One Presumption

Except for fraud and *all* other penalties, we go along with the thesis that the IRS is presumed correct (initially) on its interpretation of a specifically identified tax law. This is a matter of practicality: not of principle. We explained the practical reasoning behind this in Chapter 6: Trial Procedure.

But **one presumption** in the IRS's favor is enough. It is a ridiculous concept of equity to let the IRS switch its tax theories around, thereby forcing the petitioner to overcome one presumption after another, and then, having done so, carry the burden of proof on one alternative after another. This is not only baffling to the petitioner, it is baffling to the court as well. Let us illustrate.

The following dialogue took place at the conclusion of Trial I, with respect to Issue II (Prototype Expenses):

THE COURT: Well, there's one thing I wanted to ask both of you, and that is I gather in the so-called development expenses, it is mainly an issue of whether they are deductible research and development expenses under Section 174 or whether they are capitalized expenditures in connection with a literary or artistic production under other sections of the Code, such as 183, 263, or 280. Is that the main issue here?

THE IRS: Your Honor, if you are offering that maybe we can reopen the evidence, perhaps the Respondent can introduce **other alternate theories**. [Emphasis added.]

PETITIONER: Your Honor, what we're really talking about is whether it's in connection with a trade or business; that is, whether it's a 162 or a 174 deduction.

THE COURT: It's just a question. Now, I'm a little bit familiar because I've had them in other connections with the method of capitalizing and computing depreciation on items that do come under the literary and artistic and so forth.

Leave it to the IRS, and they'll keep the alternate-theory quibbling going on indefinitely.

The IRS is supposed to be a knowledgeable and responsible agency. If it is, then it should be held to a higher adversarial standard than other adversaries in legal disputes. As such, it should be allowed no more than one presumption of correctness, and that one must be stated fully and explicitly in its Notice of Deficiency.

To correct the inequity that has been allowed so long, an additional subsection should be added to Section 7453: Rules of Practice, Procedures, and Evidence (before the Tax Court). Add subsection 7453(b): ONE PRESUMPTION OF CORRECTNESS ONLY. Its wording might read as—

The IRS shall be allowed one presumption of correctness of its determination of a deficiency (not penalty). After that, should the IRS switch to an alternate theory of any kind, no presumption shall prevail, and all burden of proof shall be on the IRS to establish its alternate theory by a preponderance of the evidence.

It's about time that tax justice be served, and that the *brother agency syndrome* between the Tax Court and the IRS be severed.

Apply "Reasonable Nexus" Standard

The problem with the Tax Court system (including the IRS) is that the judges of taxpayers have seldom, if ever, suffered the hard knocks and uncertainties of being in a trade or business of their own. The judges approach the business world with an academic and hypothetical frame of mind. They deliberately set aside practical reasoning and common sense. Theory and sophistication in their written decisions is their pressing goal. At times, they glorify in academic nonsense.

With respect to Issue II (Prototype Expenses), for example, the Trial I judge (a female) agonized over what trade or business the petitioner was in. She also agonized over whether or not the verified expenditures for prototype demonstration samples were "in connection with" the petitioner's trade or business. To clear the way for her hypothetical analysis, she ignored entirely the petitioner's arguments (in his briefs) that he could not have developed a complete press-ready tax book on a 2-1/2-inch computer disk, without going through the painstaking preparation of hard copy samples "the old-fashioned way." It was obvious that she could not comprehend the 25-volume series of tax books on computer disks being undertaken. From her professional biography, she was an attorney with the IRS for 23 years, and was a Tax Court judge for 27 years. Not one day in her life had she experienced the uncertainty of developing a new, marketable product.

Consequently, she rationalized that the petitioner was in **two** separate trades or businesses. One business was that of being a tax return preparer; the other was that of being a tax book author. Never mind that as a tax preparer he received CPE (continuing professional education) licensing credits for authoring tax books.

Never mind that the information and experiences in his tax books were derived from his 20 years of helping tax clients. The two businesses were as different as night from day, she alleged.

The academic clincher for the court was that the expenditures were not technological in nature, because books had been published for 500 years. She took refuge in an IRS regulation which uses the phrase: "in the laboratory **or** experimental sense." She forgot to note the word "or" in this phrase. The petitioner pointed this out in his briefs, and cited other Tax Court cases where the word "experimental" does not rule out nontechnological and nonlaboratory expenditures. As long as there is some uncertainty of end-product success, the expenditures incurred can be classed as "experimental."

The court's reasoning above was unnecessarily strained. It goes beyond the bounds of Congressional intent for a reasonable (practical) interpretation of applicable tax law. To brake this pattern of academia in Tax Court proceedings, another new subsection needs to be added to the above-referenced Section 7453: Rules of Practice, Procedure, and Evidence. We suggest subsection 7453(c): REASONABLE NEXUS STANDARD. Such a subsection might read as—

Whenever it has been established that the taxpayer has indeed incurred the expenditures claimed, the Court shall apply a "reasonable nexus" standard when interpreting the applicable law on which the taxpayer relies. The Court shall not strain to arrive at a hypothetical-type decision that is devoid of practicality and common sense.

Correct "Capitalization" Inequities

The concept of capitalization versus expensing certain costs is a hypocritical stance and old-hat trick by the IRS. Sooner or later, all verifiable business costs expended are allowed. By "capitalizing" them, the revenue is front loaded and the deductions are "skewed backwards" (as we presented in Figure 10.2). It's a revenue scam where the IRS skims off the top and rakes in statutory interest and penalties along the way.

The scam works like this—

1. There is a phantom up-front deficiency created for which a tax assessment is made [Revenue 1].
2. This deficiency is subjected to the 20% accuracy-related penalty [Revenue 2].
3. On the deficiency and penalty, statutory interest (called "underpayment interest": Sec. 6601) is paid to the IRS [Revenue 3].
4. The underpayment interest is no longer deductible, whereas formerly it was [Revenue 4].
5. When the skewed backend writeoffs do occur, the deduction benefits therefrom are lower [Revenue 5].
6. Should the skewed backend writeoffs cause an over-payment, statutory interest (called "overpayment interest": Sec. 6611) is paid by the IRS. This interest, however, is includible as income which is taxable [Revenue 6].

In Chapter 10 re Issue IV, we presented testimony on the creation of phantom deficiencies in the early years and overpayments in later years, for petitioner's Schedule C Issue II expenses. At the time, the trial judge seemed to understand what was taking place. Yet, when he rendered his memorandum decision, he agreed totally with the IRS. That is, Court-induced phantom accounting changes can indeed produce "legitimate" deficiencies, statutory interest, and penalties. This is justice?

We can level the statutory interest playing field with the following amendments to the tax code, namely:

Sec. 6601(a)(2) — Treatment as Expense.
Any interest paid under this section as the consequence of a Tax Court decision shall be treated as a deductible expense under section 212 in connection with the determination, collection, or refund of any tax. Where appropriate, such interest shall be treated as a deductible expense under section 162 in connection with the trade or business of the taxpayer.

Sec. 6611(a)(2) — Treatment as Refund.
Any interest received under this section as the consequence
of a Tax Court decision shall be treated as a refund of tax which
is not includible in gross income under Section 61.

Make Certain Awards Automatic

We're not through with leveling the playing field yet. There is a
matter of attorney fees and other litigation costs. It costs a lot of
money to go into Tax Court, especially when fraud is alleged. If the
IRS doesn't win 100%, an allocable portion of the petitioner's
attorney fees should be reimbursed automatically.

For Issues I, II, and III, the attorney fees and costs paid by the
petitioner for Trials I and II totaled $92,278. The existing law on
recoverability of attorney fees is IR Code Section 7430: Awarding
of Costs and Certain Fees. Subsection (a) thereof reads in part—

In any . . . proceeding . . . in connection with the determination,
collection, or refund of any tax, interest, or penalty . . ., the
prevailing party **may be awarded**—
(1) reasonable administrative costs . . ., and
(2) reasonable litigation costs in connection with such
court proceeding. [Emphasis added.]

Furthermore, subsection 7430(c)(4)(A) requires that the
prevailing party—

Establish that the position of the [IRS] *in the proceeding was*
not substantially justified . . . with respect to—
(i) the amount in controversy, or
(ii) the most significant issue or set of issues presented.

All of which means that in addition to prevailing in a Tax Court
proceeding itself, the petitioner must further prove that the IRS was
"not substantially justified" in its actions. This is a totally separate
and additional burden of proof on the petitioner. Consequently,
Section 7430 is another one of those pernicious loopholes through
which the IRS can escape scot free.

Sections 7430(a) and (c) have been repeatedly tested in Tax Court post-trial motions. Most said motions are denied. The Tax Court, it appears, just doesn't want to ruffle the feathers of the IRS. It uses its discretionary escape hatch in the phrase "may be awarded." This phrase should be amended to: "SHALL be awarded" . . . so as to be mandatory.

Still further, subsection 7430(c)(4)(A) should be amended to be more objective, namely—

The "prevailing party" shall be—
- *(i) he who prevails in a fraud issue, in which case all litigation costs shall be awarded, or*
- *(ii) he who prevails by more than 50% of the amount of deficiency and penalty in controversy, in which case the allocable portion of litigation costs shall be awarded.*

Stop Punishing New Ideas

The IRS is a self-proclaimed punitive agency in addition to its charter to collect revenue. It passes its own character judgment on taxpayers, and then proceeds to heap punishment — pyramid style — from its menu of 55 authorized penalties. Anyone who does not agree with the IRS or who comes forth with a new idea affecting tax administration is pronounced a "tax protester." Then penalty pyramiding is imposed.

The Internal Revenue Code consists of (approximately) 1,800 sections of tax law. These are primary sections only. This number does not include the multitude of subsections and sub-subsections. Yet, nowhere in this vast array of tax law does the phrase "tax protester" appear. This characterization of a taxpayer is solely a fiction created by the IRS itself. When punishing an individual on this basis, it is operating beyond the law . . . extraconstitutionally.

Still, the IRS, together with the Tax Court, could become constructive instrumentalities in our system of government. Take the case of Issue I previously. This was an idea whose time had come (the voluntary renunciation of Social Security benefits by eligible senior citizens), which could save the nation billions of dollars annually. If only 1% of the 36,000,000 social security recipients renounced their benefits as a public gift, the 5-year savings to the U.S. Treasury would exceed 16 billion dollars ($16,000,000,000). These computations, and a proposed new tax code section 1404 with respect thereto, were sent to members of Congress, to officials in the Social Security Administration (as depicted in Figure 9.1), and were included in the volumes of documentary evidence before the Tax Court. So, too, was a notarized request to the President that he direct the IRS and Treasury Department to review and study the idea on its economic merits and benefits to the country.

What happened to the idea?

The IRS slapped a fraud penalty on the proposer, labeled him a tax protester, and forced him into spending $92,278 in attorney fees for Tax Court proceedings. No in-depth studies or analyses were made by the IRS. The Tax Court instantly sided with the IRS that the idea was frivolous, protestive, outrageous, and preposterous . . . and imposed alternative penalties on the proposer.

We truly have a long way to go before satisfactory tax justice is achieved in the United States. Tax Court judges could significantly help in this regard. Instead of acting as IRS protectors, they could act more as taxpayer advocates. They could do so by taking the initiative to introduce constructive changes in tax law and in TC procedures. But don't get your hopes up too high.

ABOUT

THE AUTHOR

Holmes F. Crouch

Born on a small farm in southern Maryland, Holmes was graduated from the U.S. Coast Guard Academy with a Bachelor's Degree in Marine Engineering. While serving on active duty, he wrote many technical articles on maritime matters. After attaining the rank of Lieutenant Commander, he resigned to pursue a career as a nuclear engineer.

Continuing his education, he earned a Master's Degree in Nuclear Engineering from the University of California. He also authored two books on nuclear propulsion. As a result of the tax write-offs associated with writing these books, the IRS audited his returns. The IRS's handling of the audit procedure so annoyed Holmes that he undertook to become as knowledgeable as possible regarding tax procedures. He became a licensed private Tax Practitioner by passing an examination administered by the IRS. Having attained this credential, he started his own tax preparation and counseling business in 1972.

In the early years of his tax practice, he was a regular talk-show guest on San Francisco's KGO Radio responding to hundreds of phone-in tax questions from listeners. He was a much sought-after guest speaker at many business seminars and taxpayer meetings. He also provided counseling on special tax problems, such as divorce matters, property exchanges, timber harvesting, mining ventures, animal breeding, independent contractors, selling businesses, and offices-at-home. Over the past 20 years, he has prepared over 9,000 tax returns for individuals, estates, and small businesses.

During the tax season of January through April, he prepares returns in a unique manner. During a single meeting, he completes the return . . . *on the spot!* The client leaves with his return signed, sealed, and in a stamped envelope. His unique approach to preparing returns and his personal interest in his clients' tax affairs have honed his professional proficiency. His expertise extends through itemized deductions, computer-matching of income sources, capital gains and losses, business expenses and cost of goods, residential rental expenses, limited and general partnership activities, closely-held corporations, to family farms and ranches.

He remembers spending 12 straight hours completing a doctor's complex return. The next year, the doctor, having moved away, utilized a large accounting firm to prepare his return. Their accountant was so impressed by the manner in which the prior return was prepared that he recommended the doctor travel the 500 miles each year to have Holmes continue doing it.

He recalls preparing a return for an unemployed welder, for which he charged no fee. Two years later the welder came back and had his return prepared. He paid the regular fee . . . and then added a $300 tip.

During the off season, he represents clients at IRS audits and appeals. In one case a shoe salesman's audit was scheduled to last three hours. However, after examining Holmes' documentation it was concluded in 15 minutes with "no change" to his return. In another instance he went to an audit of a custom jeweler that the IRS dragged out for more than six hours. But, supported by Holmes' documentation, the client's return was accepted by the IRS with "no change."

Then there was the audit of a language translator that lasted two full days. The auditor scrutinized more than $1.25 million in gross receipts, all direct costs, and operating expenses. Even though all expensed items were documented and verified, the auditor decided that more than $23,000 of expenses ought to be listed as capital items for depreciation instead. If this had been enforced it would have resulted in a significant additional amount of tax. Holmes strongly disagreed and after many hours explanation got the amount reduced by more than 60% on behalf of his client.

He has dealt extensively with gift, death and trust tax returns. These preparations have involved him in the tax aspects of wills, estate planning, trustee duties, probate, marital and charitable bequests, gift and death exemptions, and property titling.

Although not an attorney, he prepares Petitions to the U.S. Tax Court for clients. He details the IRS errors and taxpayer facts by citing pertinent sections of tax law and regulations. In a recent case involving an attorney's ex-spouse, the IRS asserted a tax deficiency of $155,000. On behalf of his client, he petitioned the Tax Court and within six months the IRS conceded the case.

Over the years, Holmes has observed that the IRS is not the industrious, impartial, and competent federal agency that its official public imaging would have us believe.

He found that, at times, under the slightest pretext, the IRS has interpreted against a taxpayer in order to assess maximum penalties, and may even delay pending matters so as to increase interest due on additional taxes. He has confronted the IRS in his own behalf on five separate occasions, going before the U.S. Claims Court, U.S. District Court, and U.S. Tax Court. These were court actions that tested specific sections of the Internal Revenue Code which he found ambiguous, inequitable, and abusively interpreted by the IRS.

Disturbed by the conduct of the IRS and by the general lack of tax knowledge by most individuals, he began an innovative series of taxpayer-oriented Federal tax guides. To fulfill this need, he undertook the writing of a series of guidebooks that provide in-depth knowledge on one tax subject at a time. He focuses on subjects that plague taxpayers all throughout the year. Hence, his formulation of the "Allyear" Tax Guide series.

The author is indebted to his wife, Irma Jean, and daughter, Barbara MacRae, for the word processing and computer graphics that turn his experiences into the reality of these publications. Holmes welcomes comments, questions, and suggestions from his readers. He can be contacted in California at (408) 867-2628, or by writing to the publisher's address.

ALLYEAR Tax Guides
by Holmes F. Crouch

Series 100 - INDIVIDUALS AND FAMILIES

BEING SELF-EMPLOYED .... T/G 101
DEDUCTING JOB EXPENSES .... T/G 102
RESOLVING DIVORCE ISSUES .... T/G 104
CITIZENS WORKING ABROAD .... T/G 105

Series 200 - INVESTORS AND BUSINESSES

INVESTOR GAINS & LOSSES .... T/G 201
HOBBY BUSINESS VENTURES .... T/G 202
STARTING YOUR BUSINESS .... T/G 203

Series 300 - RETIREES AND ESTATES

DECISIONS WHEN RETIRING .... T/G 301
WRITING YOUR WILL .... T/G 303
YOUR EXECUTOR DUTIES .... T/G 304
TRUSTS AND TRUSTEES .... T/G 305

Series 400 - OWNERS AND SELLERS

RENTAL REAL ESTATE .... T/G 401
SELLING YOUR HOME .... T/G 403
SELLING YOUR BUSINESS .... T/G 405

Series 500 - AUDITS AND APPEALS

KEEPING GOOD RECORDS .... T/G 501
WINNING YOUR AUDIT .... T/G 502
YOUR TAXPAYER RIGHTS .... T/G 503
GOING INTO TAX COURT .... T/G 505

Contact your local bookstore or library for any of the above.

For a free 8-page catalog,
or information about the above titles, contact:

ALLYEAR Tax Guides

20484 Glen Brae Drive, Saratoga, CA 95070

Phone: (408) 867-2628   Fax: (408) 867-6466